The Sacred World of Temples

The Sacred World of Temples

Dr. Adyasha Das

BLACK EAGLE BOOKS
2021

BLACK EAGLE BOOKS

USA address:
7464 Wisdom Lane
Dublin, OH 43016

India address:
E/312, Trident Galaxy, Kalinga Nagar,
Bhubaneswar-751003, Odisha, India

E-mail: info@blackeaglebooks.org
Website: www.blackeaglebooks.org

First International Edition published by
Black Eagle Books, 2021

THE SACRED WORLD OF TEMPLES
by Dr. Adyasha Das

Copyright © **Dr. Adyasha Das**

All rights reserved. No part of this publication may be reproduced, stored in a retrieval system, or transmitted, in any form or by any means, electronic, mechanical, photocopying, recording or otherwise without the prior permission of the publisher.

Interior Design: Ezy's Publication

ISBN- 978-1-64560-143-2 (Paperback)
Library of Congress Control Number: 2021930022

Printed in United States of America

Akshaya Chandra Ray

For Dearest Bapi,

    For always believing in me....
    My love for you transcends Time.

Foreword

One God, many faces.
One family, many races.
One truth, many paths.
One heart, many complexions.
One light, many reflections.
One world, many imperfections.
ONE.
We are all one,
But many.

— **Suzy Kassem**, Rise Up and Salute the Sun

The fascination with temples probably began when I was a child. Childhood memories are precious and have had a profound impact on my life and creations. Memories of childhood are the dreams that we never forget. Whenever I walk down memory lane, I stop at this quaint gate, and a swarm of butterflies burst out in all their colour to paint my world with innocence, the honeysuckle smell of love dripping all over me. Those were the days of being unafraid of anything, everything because my father held my hand .Far from being cloistered, I had the freedom to discover the beauty all around- the colourful butterflies that blew like flowers through the golden air, wild flowers with exotic names, and the diamond drops that rained and cleansed everything. My father was posted as an engineer at Dhenkanal. He was religious and believed in visiting God in his abode every now and then. The first temple I remember visiting with him was the famous Kapilash temple at Dhenkanal. Those were fun trips for us. We were more interested in the jeep ride, the unknown roads and Ma's tasty food than the place of worship. But once inside the temple, with the hymns and mantras filling the air, I felt at peace. I had no inkling then that those experiences were the beginning of my spiritual sojourns later in life.

I have lost track of how many temples I must have visited with him till the last temple visit to Jagannath Dham, Puri. I have missed him intensely through each word I have put together for this book.

The pre-historic man worshipped different elements of nature for fear of their potential to inflict calamities or curse as well as in reverence for the benefits he received from them. His sense of gratitude went to the extent of bestowing godhood of such forces of nature as the sun, rain, river, forest, mountain, animal and plants etc. Gradually, temples and other religious institutions were created and elaborate rituals as well as functions were performed there to appease the presiding deities. He offered them specific materials of his choice including leaf, flower, fruit, seeds etc. and also used different plant products in those religious activities.

The temple has always been regarded as a sacred place in Hinduism. "Sacred" is derived from the Latin root sacrare (*http://www.merriam-webster.com/dictionary/sacred*), which means to dedicate exclusively for the service of the gods. A "sanctum" is a place of inviolable privacy. On the other hand, "profane", derived from the Latin profanus, is that which relates to the uninitiated or ordinary life. (http://www.merriam-webster.com/dictionary/sacred)

The institutions of temples and their traditions play a vital role in the socio-cultural landscapes of many societies today. The "sacredness" in Hindu temples is interpreted from several aspects - with respect to physical attributes and spatial arrangements, which channelize the focus of devotees on the sacredness contained within the temple, in contrast to the "profaneness" of the surrounding world. Divinity is a concept much emphasized in Hinduism and other world religions. The word 'divine', over time has been associated with God and supernatural powers. Ancient Indian texts elaborate about divinities with regard to the many Gods of the Hindu pantheon. They, in turn have influenced the myths of later times and modern religions. Despite several million gods that are venerated in Hinduism, the high priests and mendicants understand and believe in the existence of One Supreme God – Brahman.

Bhubaneswar offers to the scholars of history and temple architecture as well as to tourists a scope to study the evolution of Kalingan style over a period of two thousand years with temples of amazing diversity in a radius of few kilometres. Both the aspects of evolution of temple architecture and the presence of variety in one place are unique in India.

The ideology behind the designing of Hindu temples is to link man with the gods. Hindu temple is the place where one can feel being close to god. It is a depiction of the macrocosm (the universe) as well as the microcosm (the inner space) and has developed over two thousand years. A large variety of Hindu temples was constructed throughout India with distinction in scale, techniques of building and particularly the deities that were worshipped, which were the result of the differences in political, cultural and prosperity between the towns and villages. The character of Hindu temples reflected local architecture styles and the material and skills to which they related. The information which survived explains that the temple building, especially in stone and brick was carried out as a result of royal patronage. Other than royal patrons, association of wealthy merchants and group of individuals played an important role in the construction of temples. (Vardia Shweta, Building a Science of Indian Temple Architecture)

The Hindu temple structure presents the significant information about the science and cosmology of the period in which they were constructed. It is a symbolism of the outer and the inner cosmos where outer cosmos is expressed in terms of various astronomical connections between the temple structure and the motions of the sun, the moon, and the planets, whereas the inner cosmos is represented in terms of the consciousness at the womb of the temple and various levels of the superstructure correspond to the levels of consciousness (Kak, 2002). In the words of Stella Kramrisch, "The temple is the concrete shape (mûrti) of the Essence; as such it is the residence and vesture of God. The masonry is the sheath (koœa) and body. The temple is the monument of manifestation."

The palpable serenity, quietude and a feeling of being elsewhere in time and space is an ethereal experience for many. There is a distinct vibration of the temples, perhaps beyond the pale of explanation by material science - the aesthetic and the psychic dimensions of being become operative. The temple is like a fixed chariot. The chariot is a moving temple. Both of them are modeled after man/woman who is a living temple. *Rathetu Bamanam drustwa punarjanmam na bidyate.* If one sees(realises) the divine in the humans(or rather embodied ones) one is liberated.

India is a land of rare splendour created by temples. Scores of man-made and natural wonders exist that go beyond scientific reasoning. Many label them as mysteries or miracles, not just structures but spiritual centers. Many of these age-old traditions are now confronted with a pragmatic society. In modern times, different studies of tourism and religion in contemporary India and Asia show the penetration of tourism into all regions, institutions, belief systems and peoples' lives. None of the religions remain untouched by the effects of commercial tourism and modern urban systems. Even those who wish to continue to worship as did their ancestors, have to worship in new contexts with visiting tourists, new spaces and modern technologies.

The new- age visitor to temple goes in search of mindfulness. Mindfulness is a practice considered to be an integral part of various religious and secular traditions. It was practiced in the East by religious and spiritual institutions, while in the West its popularity was primarily due to particular people and secular institutions.

"Mindfulness has been intertwined with Hinduism for millennia. From the Bhagavad Gita's discussions of yoga to Vedic meditation, the history of Hinduism reads in part like a history of mindfulness."(https://positivepsychology.com/)

The temples, considered to be the primary religious organizations, are changing roles to fit the new social trend. In the past, temples were the centre of community lifestyles and religious activity. Creating cultural identities enhances cultural capital value, capturing the tourists' faith through interaction with respected monk or priests, combining and adapting religious beliefs to the local faiths, setting up the temple' tourism landmark, and building a unique tradition of the temple and the community.

One of my ongoing research projects attempts to ascertain non-religious and religious tourism trends in Puri, Odisha as evident among an increasing number of visitors to Puri, both from proximity states and from further afield in India. Visitors to Puri are of religious and non-religious appearance and growth of both types are reported. Religious tourism centres on temples and religious festivals, while non-religious tourism includes beach-related recreation as well as cultural and nature-based excursions, including nearby Konark and Chilika Lake

This book is a collection of experiences of my visits and travels to different temples and temple towns over time in India and abroad. It is a travel account of temples and not a book of history. Needless to say, there are many more that will probably run into another volume. My research in the area of cultural tourism intensified the interest for visiting and understanding spiritual spaces. Most of the photographs are mine and some belong to my dear students. I thank Debika Mondal, Debabrata Ghadei, Mukesh Chandray & Baishnabi Behera for allowing me to use their creative photographs. My family, Lalit and Ishani, share my interest for travel and most of these visits have been with them. Had it not been for them, I may not have seen so many beautiful temples. Special thanks to my mother, Pratibha Ray, who has been a constructive critic at all times. Her experience and insights have helped me greatly. My sincere thanks to Sankar Narayan Mallik for his valuable inputs and support in finalizing this book. His in-depth analysis and reflections helped me fine-tune certain aspects. My sincere thanks to Satya Pattanaik and Black Eagles Books for helping me realize my fond dream in bringing out this special book. I have been sharing these temple travel accounts as a serial, *"The Temple Trail"* in social media. The interest and appreciation of my readers made me contemplate the idea of putting it together in the form of a book. Mostly, I pay reverence to the unseen force which made me discover the world in myself through these temple visits.

CONTENTS

Temples of Odisha

Lingaraja Temple	21
Markandeswara Temple	24
Sisireswar Temple	25
Vaital/Baitala Temple	26
Taleswara Temple	27
The Laxmaneswar Temple	28
The Bharateswar Temple	29
Shatrughaneswara Temple	30
Mukteshwar Temple	31
Brahmeswara Temple	32
Raja Rani Temple	33
Megheswar Temple	34
Bakreswar Temple	35
Rameshwar Deula/Kusakeswara Temple	36
Bhringesvara Temple	37
Sari Deul Temple	38
Viswanath Temple	40
Ganga Yamuna Temple	41
Uttareswar Temple	42
Swarna Jaleswar Temple	43
Tirtheswara Temple	44
Mohini Temple	45
The Bindusagar Temple Tank	46
SwapneswarTemple	47
Alarnath Temple	49
Konark Sun Temple	51
Shree Jagannath Temple	53
Kapilash Temple	55
Cuttack Chandi Temple	56
Dakshinakali Temple	57
Maa Kandhuni Devi temple	58
Buddhanath Temple	60
Gopinath Jiu (Gopaljiu) Temple	62
Chandaneshwar Shiva Temple	63
Ramachandi Temple	64

Maa Bhagabati Temple	66
BhabakundaleswarTemple	67
Maa Biraja Temple	68
The Leaning Temple of Huma	69
Prasanna Purusottam Dev Temple	71
Maa Sarala Temple	72
Maa Tarini Temple	73
Narayani Temple	74
The forgotten village temples	75

Temples of Assam

Kamakhya Temple	78
Sidheswar Devalaya	79
Kedar Temple	80
Shri Kedareshwar Shivalay	81
Hayagriv Madhav Temple	82

Temples of Tripura

The Gunabati Group of Temples	84
Bhuvaneshwari Temple	85
Tripureshwari Temple	86

Temples of South India

Shore Temple	88
The Airavateswara Temple	89
The Brihadeeshwara Temple	90
Swamimalai Swaminathaswamy Temple	91
Shiva Temple	92

Temples of Rajasthan

The Chaturmukha Jain Temple	94
Sahastra/Saas Baahu Temple	95
Eklingji Temple	96

Temples of Varanasi

The Ghats of Varanasi	98
Kal Bhairav Temple	100
Shri Vishwanath Mandir	101
Durga Mandir	102
Sarnath: Buddhist Monastery...	103

Chausathi Yogini Temples

Chousati (Chausatthi) Ghat, Varanasi	106
Yogmaya Temple	107
Chausath Yogini Temple, Khajuraho	108
The Chausath Yogini Temple, Morena	110
Chausathi Yogini Temple, Hirapur. Bhubaneswar	112

Chausathi Yogini Temple, Ranipur Jharial, Odisha	114
The Temples of Bagan, Myanmar	115
Cultural Landscapes: Bagan Temples	116
Mahabodhi Temple	117
Nanpaya Temple	118
Payanthonzu Temple	119
Ananda Temple	120
Htilominlo Temple	121
Ananda Temple	122
North Guni Temple	123
Gub Yauk Gyi - 12th century cave temple, Bagan	124
The Temples of Yangon	127
Shwedagon Pagoda, Yangon	128

Temples of Cambodia

Angkor Wat	130
Ta Prohm Temple	138
Banteay Srei	139
Bayon Temple	140
The Devata yogini trail- Cambodia	142

Temples of Indonesia

Borobudur Temple Compounds	144
Candi Prambanan Temple	145

Temples of Egypt

The Great Sphinx of Giza	147
Temple of Luxor & Karnak	149
Karnak Temple	150

Temples of Sri Lanka

The Temple of the Sacred Tooth Relic	152

The Forgotten Goddess

The Forgotten Goddesses Vinayaki	154
The Forgotten Goddess Varuni	155
Forgotten Goddess USHA	156
The Mother Goddess	157
The Goddess Concept	158
The author in different Temples	159

I love you when you bow in your mosque, kneel in your temple, pray in your church. For you and I are sons of one religion, and it is the spirit.

Khalil Gibran

Jagannath Temple, Puri
Drone shot: **Debabrata Ghadei**

Temples of Odisha

"The longest journey is the journey inward."
Dag Hammarskjold, Markings

Lingaraja Temple
Old Town, Bhubaneshwar

Deity: Shiva as Lingaraja, Adidev
(Maheswara, Tribhuvaneshwara, Bhubaneswar),
Vishnu as Adi Narayana, (Harihara)
Bhuvaneshvari form of Parvati (consort)

On the summit of eternity
A soul of infinities
Mystic loneliness,
Bare ecstasy.

The Lingaraja temple, a symbol of Odisha's rich heritage, is dedicated to Shiva and is one of the oldest temples in Bhubaneswar. It is one of the major tourist attractions of the state, specifically for the religious/spiritual tourists.

One of the largest temples, the height of its imposing central tower is 180 ft. The temple, symbolizing the essence of the Kalinga architecture is believed to have been built by the kings of Somavamsi dynasty, with later expansions and augmentations by the rulers of the Ganga dynasty. Built in the Deula style, it has four components - vimana (the sanctum), jagamohana (assembly hall), natamandira (festival hall) and bhoga-mandapa (hall of offerings). The temple complex includes 50 other shrines, enclosed by a large compound wall. There is evidence to indicate that part of the temple was built during the sixth century CE as mentioned in ancient Sanskrit texts. Shivaratri is the main festival celebrated which attracts thousands of devotees and tourists. The popular legend goes that Lord Shiva confided to Goddess Parvati that he prefers Bhubaneshwar (Ekamra Kshetra as per Bhrama Purana) more than Banaras. Parvati decided to see the place in the guise of a cowherd. Shiva then created a lake Bindu Sagar to quench her thirst and resided there as Lingaraja.

Throughout the temple, images and sculptures of Vishnu and Siva are depicted as Harihara, the form of Vishnu and Siva together as one equal god where they are worshipped as Hari (Vishnu) and Hara (Siva). Although mainly dedicated to Siva, the Lingaraj temple worships the two gods as equals; thus, each gate into

Lingaraj delineate the gatekeepers of the deva. This is shown by the portrayals of Jaya and Vijaya on one gate for Vishnu, Nandi and Bhrkuti on the other for Siva. Seen amongst many of the other structures outside the temples is the depiction of the vehicles of Siva, Nandi, and Vishnu, Garuda, next to Harihara sitting in dvibhanga pose (Mishra 147).

The temple represents a unique blend of Shaivism with Vaishnavism. At the top of the temple, there is half of a trident (trishul) combined with half of a wheel (chakra). In worshipping the main deity, both Bilwa/Bel and Basil/Tulsi leaves are offered.

Dr. K. C. Panigrahi opines that some of the temples, even small ones and that of Bhubaneswari may have preceded the main temple. These have been situated in the premises of the temple.

Markandeswara Temple
Near Bindusagar, Bhubaneswar

Built by the artistic Bhaumakaras, this rare temple is built in the Kalingan Pancharatha style. The walls are exquisitely engraved with intricate sculptures, from the eight grahas on the door jamb to the ten - armed Nataraja images within the chaitya windows. The temple has sculptures of varying themes, ranging from the mundane and divine - erotic sculptures to men in a drunken state, linga worship etc.

The legends of Puranas indicate that great saint Markandeya, during his visit to the Ekamra Kshetra established this temple and a linga which came to be worshipped as Markandeswara. Markandeswara temple is located at the edge of the Bindu Sagar tank.

Sisireswar Temple
Old Town, Bhubaneswar

This temple, located along with Vaital Deul is dedicated to Lord Shiva. With splendid carvings on the wall, this 8th Century place of worship is a pilgrim site and place of worship. A Shaivite monument, it has Lord Shiva as its chief deity. Other deities such as goddess Kapali Kali are also found in the temple. It is considered a significant landmark in the evolution of temple architecture in Odisha. The temple comprises of the deula (now without the crowning members and the upper part of the gandi) and a rectangular Jagamohana The deula, is of the pancharatha plan. The niches of the central projections reveal forms of Siva including Aja¬Ekapada, Ardhanarisvara and Hari-Hara.

Vaital/Baitala Temple
Old Town, Bhubaneswar

The unique Vaital/Baital Temple is a sacred Tantric Pith dedicated to Goddess Chamunda. The khakara style Hindu temple, the exquisite panels of deities, the eight-armed Chandika all make this Shakti shrine one of its kind. There are fifteen sculptures adorning the Jagamohana. The ferocious figure of Chamunda is surrounded by Matrika figures like Brahmani, Mahesvari, Kaumari, Vaishnavi, Varahi and Aindri. Virabhadra is also found along with the Matrika figures. Researchers and historians associate the Vaital temple with the practice of Tantra connected with strange carvings in the sanctum and the presence of Kapa?ini, the terrifying form of goddess Durga. Thus, Baita?a Deu?a is regarded as a Shakti shrine.

Taleswara Temple
Old Town, Bhubaneswar

Though situated close to Bindusagar, I had a tough time getting some information from the locals about the exact location of Taleswara temple. However, I managed to get to the temple ultimately, all spruced up after its restoration. Reduced to ruins due to sheer neglect, the temple has got a face-lift, thanks to the efforts of Intach.

Famed to have been constructed by the Bhaumakaras, the unique iconography and architecture reflect a significant Buddhist influence and the architectural style is Kalingan. Beautiful sculptures from the temple now find place in the Odisha State Museum. Bearing distinct similarities to the Vaitala temple, this is yet another ancient temple that whispers the tale of Odisha's glorious heritage.

The Laxmaneswar Temple
Bhubaneswar

The colossal ruins of the Laxmaneswara temple (6th century A.D.) lie in the heart of the temple city. Flanked by Bharateswar and Shatrughaneswar temples, they are referred to as the Laxmaneswar group of temples. As I strolled inside the premises, it was difficult to believe that the temple complex lies in the heart of the town, opposite a modern row of shops. The Laxmaneswar Group of temples, all the three, in their simple structures of a temple building without mukhasala or any accretion of that type is indicative of the earlier stage of temple architecture. It may also be noted the builders, the famed Sailodbhava dynasty was also credited with the construction of Angkor Wat in Cambodia. Another interesting point to note is the supremacy of Shiva (vis-à-vis) Vishnu; Shiva has been depicted as the Lord of Rama and his three brothers. Incidentally, the Rameswar Temple is in front of this trinity of temples even as the style and time may be different.

The Bharateswar Temple
Bhubaneshwar

Bharateswar Temple, built in the 6th Century under the patronage of the Sailodbhava dynasty, is named after Bharata, Lord Rama's brother. Serene in its simplicity, it shines despite the relative anonymity. An epitome of the old Kalingan style of shrine architecture, this temple is dedicated to Lord Shiva. Bharateswar Temple is among the earliest existing temples as indicated by its intricate design, specially a Rekha vimana. Despite being situated very close to other famous temples, it retains its splendour and so is a favourite haunt of tourists. I was struck by the quietude, despite the hustle and bustle of Old Town all around.

Shatrughaneswara Temple
Bhubaneshwar

This temple, (6th century A.D.) is part of a cluster of three temples, along with the temples of Lakshmanesvara and Bharatesvara. Built during the Sailodbhava rule, it is one of the oldest temples. The sculptures on the monuments are similar to the Dasavatara temple at Deogarh. Lord Shiva reigns supreme in these three temples.

Mukteshwar Temple
Bhubaneshwar

There are temples which leave you wishing to be a part of the past they were built in, and then there are temples where the very entrance takes your breath away. Mukteshwar Temple, located in the heart of Odisha's capital, Bhubaneshwar, has an arched gateway that is far more famous than the temple itself. It is an important religious and historical site of Odisha. Dedicated to Lord Shiva, the temple offers a serene and tranquil ambiance. Rightly described as a jewel of Odishan architecture, it has exquisite carvings and is famed for its captivating and enthralling sculptures- graceful nayikas, naga-nagi, and beautiful Saptamatrikas. A popular tourist point, it is also the backdrop for the famous Mukteshwar festival.

Brahmeswara Temple
Bhubaneshwar

This temple was built in 1060 AD by Kolavaidevi, the mother of Somavamsi King Udyotakesari, The temple exteriors are intricately inlaid with many forms of Shiva. This includes Ajaikapada, Nataraja, Ardhanarisvara and Bhairava. Along with the main shrine, there are four smaller shrines in the corners. Thus, it is rightly known as a panchatanaya temple. The pidhajagamohana and rekhadeula are inter-connected. The jagamohana has two balustrade windows ornamented with carvings of women. The deula has multiple, small angasikharas as relief work.

Raja Rani Temple
Bhubaneshwar

This temple is not only considered to have immense religious significance but is famous for its sculptural excellence. Dating back to the 11th century, it is constructed from a particular type of sandstone called Rajarani. The temple is famous for its elegant Digapalakas and Nayikas. Layers of angasikharas containing miniature rekha temples distinguish the Temple gandi while two balustrade windows accentuate the Jagamohana. The Department of Tourism, Government of Odisha organizes a Rajarani Music Festival at the temple every year from January 18 to 20 focusing on showcasing all three styles of classical music – Hindustani, Carnatic and Odissi. Musicians from different parts of the country perform during the three-day festival.

Megheswar Temple
Bhubaneshwar

This is an intricately carved 12th century Hindu temple dedicated to Lord Shiva. The arched gate, intricate stone engravings & exquisite wall carvings make it unique. Towards the close of the twelfth century, Swapneswardev, the Commander-in-chief of the Ganga Dynasty built Megheswar temple. Megheswar is a relatively small temple, but with a unique look, particularly its platypus/turtle shaped-dome. With the distinct Saptaratha architecture form, the temple is decorated with magnificent carvings of dancers, animals, birds and flowers. Located at Tankapani Road, Bhubaneswar, the temple complex also has the equally ornate Bhaskareswar and Brahmeswar.

Bakreswar Temple
Bhubaneshwar

Like many ancient temples, Bakreswar is not a living temple. Relatively simple, with not much ornamentation, the temple loses its grace due to the encroachment of residential buildings. With reference to the Triratha, Pancharatha and Saptaratha temples, Bakreswar is the lone temple which is Navaratha, one and only one among the temples extant in the City of Temples.

The unique saptha-ratha plan of this temple reflects that in the area between kanika and pratiratha a narrow paga is inserted which has all the patterns and elements of bada and the gandi above. This design converts the saptha-ratha into a constrained nava-ratha pattern. None of the niches have images at present.

Rameshwar Deula/Kusakeswara Temple
Bhubaneshwar

Legend goes that when a victorious Lord Rama was returning from Lanka after defeating Ravana, Goddess Sita asked to worship Shiva at this point. So Rama built a Linga for her worship. Traditionally during Ashokashtami, which is celebrated a day before Rama Navami , Lord Lingaraja comes to this temple by a large chariot called Rukuna Rath and stays for four days. The temple dates back to 9th century.

Bhringesvara Temple
Bhubaneshwar

This ancient temple is situated on the foothills of Dhauli on the left bank of the river Daya, in the south-eastern outskirts of Bhubaneswar. The presiding deity is a circular yoni pitha with a hole at the centre. It has been renovated entirely by employing the earlier materials and sandstone. This temple is now under the protection of Odisha State Archaeology Department. Various rituals and festivals are observed like Shivaratri, Kartika purnima, Raja Sankranti, Jalasaya ceremony. Social functions like thread ceremony, mundana, and marriage ceremony are performed. Village public meetings are held in the premises.

Sari Deul Temple
Bhubaneshwar

The Sari Deul, an ancient shrine situated in Bhubaneswar Old Town Area, is an outstanding example of a Sapta-Ratha temple, noted for its intricate carvings. As I walked up the nondescript lane leading to this rare wonder, I was struck by the relative anonymity of the location. Surrounded by houses and encroachment on all sides, this exquisite piece of architecture lies forgotten, in a state of neglect. I spotted some young girls living in the house across the temple and asked them if they knew something about the temple. They smiled and said it was Sari Deul, that's all.

The presiding deity here is Goddess Parvati, the consort of Lord Shiva. Its art and architecture are indicative of the Ganga period. The temple has a narrow courtyard, enclosed by a low compound wall. The ornamented balustrade windows on the south side have intricate carvings

of dancers and musicians. The niche above the south window depicts a royal procession with the king seated on an elephant, surrounded by infantry, cavalry and elephants. Sari Temple is one of the many 13th century Eastern Ganga era temples scattered around the Old town area of Bhubaneswar, between and around the compound of the famed Lingaraj temple and Bindu Sagar tank. Sari is tucked away in the narrow alleyway, close to the Papanasini temple.

    Sari Temple and adjacent free-standing Rekha Deul (sanctum tower), are also referred to as Suka-Sari. A piece of architecture can have integrity. As I sat in the courtyard amidst the sheen of twilight spilling all around, I marvelled at the mighty perspective of eternity as depicted by the temple....of infinite beginnings and endless ends!

Viswanath Temple
Bhubaneshwar

Dedicated to Viswanath, this living temple is situated close to the Lingaraj temple. The temple is enveloped by the imposing Lingaraj temple wall. Though the architectural style is Kalingan, it is a relatively modern construction.

Ganga Yamuna Temple
Bhubaneshwar

The ancient city of Ekamra/Bhubaneswar is a prominent Shaiva site with hundreds of Shiva temples. Ganga Yamuna is a non-descript, quietly elusive temple in the Old Town area. It was extremely quiet that afternoon when I had visited. Just a few locals hanging out. I went around the small, quaint temple and saw the priceless statues, ancient and rare. The Ganga Yamuna tank looked very much in need of cleaning and care. Nevertheless, it had its holy tag, enough to attract tourists. I found it perfect for meditation, especially as it was very quiet and afforded complete solitude.

One God, many faces
One truth, many paths.....

Uttareswar Temple
Old Town, Bhubaneswar

This ancient temple is situated near the famed Bindusagar Lake. It is popularly believed that the gods play water sports here. There is a pond named Godavari Kunda located close to the temple Uttareswara and legend goes that taking a dip in it equals a trip to Godavari. The deul and jagamohana of the temple are similar to that of the Parsurameswar Temple. The images of Parsva-Devatas (the secondary gods) and Lord Kartikeya are unique in their appearance. I went to visit this special shrine with my daughter on a lonely afternoon.  To our utter surprise, the temple area, the sacred space, was being used for Yoga classes. A group of local ladies were the students.

A sacred place is first of all a defined place, a space distinguished from other spaces. The rituals that people either practice at a place or direct toward it mark its sacredness and differentiate it from other defined spaces. I asked the women why they had decided to choose this sacred temple for their Yoga practice. They thought this place as ideal as it was mostly deserted, open and secluded. Also, they admitted that Yoga was secondary and their meeting together was the primary reason.

What a redefinition of sacred space!

Swarna Jaleswar Temple
Bhubaneswar

One of the ancient temples of Odisha, the Swarna Jaleswar temple remains hidden in a narrow alley, in close proximity to the Lingaraj temple. Anonymous and forgotten, it lies neglected. On the northern niche of the temple is a scene of Lord Shiva's marriage. The walls also exhibit scenes from Ramayana & Mahabharata in a sunken panel running around the Vimana and the transition between the Vada and the Sikhara.

I visited with a group of students from the college where I work and together we cleaned the area which was densely covered with weeds and wild plants. Despite the ruined condition of the temple, the beauty of the statues was striking.

Tirtheswara Temple
Old Town, Bhubaneswar

The beauty of the ancient temples dotting the old town area of Bhubaneswar is unparalleled. However, the encroachments on either side of the temples rob them of their aesthetic grace. The 14th century Tirtheswara Shiva temple attracts tourists and locals alike. Situated near the Bindusagar tank on the Talabazar Road, archaeologists believe the Tirtheswara temple was built during the last phase of reign of the Ganga rulers. Sandstone has been used for the temple structure, while the foundation has been made of laterite.

Devoid of intricate sculptural embellishments, the striking feature about the site is its lofty built. However, a number of buildings surround three sides of the temple. On two sides, private buildings and shops have come up while an old Dharamshala stands on another side. Plastered and painted in red, the temple is buried at the base. It was renovated few years ago and the local residents look after it.

Mohini Temple
Bindusagar Area, Bhubaneshwar

With Chamunda as the reigning deity, this quaint temple lies almost incognito between buildings on the southern bank of Bindusagar. As the shrine of one of the Ashtachandi's, it is an embodiment of power that has been redefined over time. Mohini Devi, the Bhaumakara queen constructed the temple as a dedication to the powerful Chamunda. The images of the parsva-devatas, Parvati, Kartikeya & Ganesha, though damaged have been satisfactorily restored. I strolled near the Mohini Ghat in front of the temple and imagined that time had retraced its steps. Without the hustle and bustle of the local bazaar, this would have been a place of serious mediation and worship. I found some young boys and girls taking pictures against the back-drop of the Mohini temple. When I spoke to them, they had no idea who the primary deity was. However, they did volunteer to take some of my pictures.

The Bindusagar Temple Tank
Old Town, Bhubaneshwar

The Bindusagar Lake, ensconced amidst a bevy of beautiful shrines, is about 1300 ft in length and 700 ft in width. Despite its proximity to crowded temples and the busy shops, it creates a tranquil and peaceful aura that immediately revitalizes the soul. The lake serves as a focal point around which numerous temples of Bhubaneshwar are located.

Each year, the idol of Lord Lingaraja (Lord Shiva), enshrined in the Lingaraja Temple, is brought to the lake for a ritual bath. It is popularly believed that a dip in the Bindu Sagar Lake washes away all sins and diseases. There is a popular myth connected with this temple tank. After defeating and destroying the demons, Goddess Parvati was thirsty and appealed to Lord Shiva. Acknowledging her prayer, Lord Shiva created this sagar to quench her thirst. However, pollution is a major problem hindering the popularity of this rare tourist spot. The lack of hygienic surroundings prevents tourists from spending longer time in this legendary spot.

Swapneswar Temple
Bankadagada, Khurda

Bankadagada, the capital city of the Shailodbhaba dynasty rulers, was once a prosperous town. Now, it remains in ruins amidst a jungle near the Salia Dam, situated at a distance of around four kms from Banpur on the NH-5 near the Chilika Lake. Archaeologists state that the Sailodbhaba rulers were powerful during the 6th to 7th century, and they perhaps initiated the culture of temple building for the first time in the state. At that time, the temples were built like an amphi-theatre as they were not covered. Later, in the 7th century, the art of temple building changed its style and the covered temples emerged. The excavated temple at Bankadagada is perhaps the one built by the successor of Pulind Sen.

The temple is a panchayatana temple, having four smaller subsidiary temples around the main temple, where a huge Shiva Linga is worshipped, as the presiding deity. Although, in ruins, it still reflects its architectural magnificence. Most of the figures carved in the temple walls are unidentified sculptures, from an earlier period of temple building. There is a big stone slab found at the entrance to the temple that contains ancient Pali inscriptions along with a huge Sahasra Linga which is worshiped inside the subsidiary temple located in the north eastern corner.

Tourists can visit the place as well as Banpur, the abode of Goddess Bhagabati. Legends say that Banasura of Lord Krishna's time was the founder of a kingdom and Banpur was its capital.

Alarnath Temple
Brahmagiri

Alarnatha Temple, dedicated to Vishnu is located in Brahmagiri, Odisha, in close proximity of Puri. Relatively isolated except the local devotees, it is sought after during the krishnapaksha of Ashadha, after the Snana Yatra when lord Jagannath cannot be seen in Puri. During this period, popularly known as Anasara (literally meaning no opportunity to see the lord of Puri), it is popularly believed that Lord Jagannath manifests as Alarnath Dev, at the Alarnath temple. The alvars also spelt as alwars, Tamil poet saints of South India preached devotion to God Vishnu and the puja was previously performed by South Indian Brahmins. Because the priests were disciples of the great spiritual teachers known as the Alvars, the deity became known as Alvarnatha ("Lord of the Alvars"), and consequently Alarnath. The present temple was built about eleven hundred years ago.

I had several interesting experiences, from being forbidden to take pictures and carry my mobile inside the temple to the priest at the Lakshmi mandir who insisted I get it back. He asked me to sit for some time in the Lakshmi Mandir as hurrying would make wealth slip away. There was also this stranger who accompanied me, stated he is not a guide, volunteered information and "prashad" and refused to take some money I offered. It was a serene afternoon and I was filled with a calmness that I had not experienced for long.

Credit: Baisnabi Behera

Konark Sun Temple
Konark

The Sun Temple at Konârk, a UNESCO world heritage site, is one of the outstanding examples of temple architecture and art as revealed in its conception, scale and proportion, and in the sublime narrative strength of its sculptural embellishment. A monumental example of the personification of divinity, it forms an invaluable link in the history of the diffusion of the cult of Surya, the Sun God.

Found in the east coast of India, black pagoda was built in the 1200 AD by Langula NarSingh Dev, the ruler of erstwhile Kalinga. It is constructed at such an angle that the first rays of light always falls on the sanctum. The temple is in the form of a chariot drawn by eight horses on twelve pairs of intricately decorated wheels. Majestic carvings adorn the wall of the main temple, and the Natya Mandap (in front of the temple). The temple is a symbol of the passage of time, which is governed by the Sun God.

Credit: Debika Mondal

Shree Jagannath Temple
Puri

The Shree Jagannath Temple is a famous Hindu temple dedicated to Jagannath, appearing as a form of Vishnu, in Puri. The temple was rebuilt on the land of an earlier temple around 10th century by King Anantavarman Chodaganga Deva, first of the Eastern Ganga dynasty. Known the world over for its annual Ratha yatra, or chariot festival, in which the three principal deities are pulled on huge and elaborately decorated temple cars, it is regarded as one of the Char Dhams of the Hindu's. Many great saints have been associated with the temple. Ramanuja established the Emar Mutt near the temple and Adi Shankaracharya established the Govardhana Mutt.

Jagannath Culture is essentially an elastic culture. Apart from influencing other cultures, it has incorporated into its fold the cultures of various faiths. Shri Jagannath is the Saura's wooden Deity without sense organs. Again, He is the Dravidian Deity with sense organs. He is the Purusottama of the Vedas and Darubrahma of the Brahmins. His rituals remind us of Dravidian customs and His festivals are of Puranic origin. Of his Mantras (incantations) OUM is Vedic and Hrim,Slim, Klim are Tantric. His Kaibalya is of Jain origin and Nirmalya is of Shaiva origin. A close observation of His worship, attire, food, rites and rituals make us conclude that Shri Jagannath culture has assimilated features from other cultures.

Lord Jagannath is identified as Bhairaba in Tantra philosophy. His consort, Bhairabi is goddess Bimala .The Bhairavi Chakra has been inscribed near the Ratna Simhasana / Vedi in the Jagannath temple. Sri Jagannath has been installed on this Srichakra. The image of Bhairava has also installed on the Ratna Simhasana. Several temple images of the Bhauma period depict Ekapada Bhairaba, carved in the form of a wooden pillar, with the big round eyes that characterize the Ugra form, a tiger skin on his hips, and the urdhvalingam like the lions at the gates of the temple.

Kapilash Temple
Dhenkanal

The temple at Kapilash, identified as the Chandrashekhar Temple is situated in the north eastern part of Dhenkanal town, Odisha. My memories of this sacred temple go back to the precious days of my childhood when Kapilash was a favourite visit, close to home. We would all pile on to my father's jeep and ride happily to the temple. There are two ways to reach the temple. The first is by climbing 1352 steps that lead through a canopy of trees to the temple. The other is through Barabanki, travelling the meandering route up the hill. King Narasinghdeva I of Ganga Dynasty constructed the temple for Sri Chandrasekhar in 1246 CE. The hallmark of the temple is its wooden Jagamohana. Several other Gods and Goddesses are worshipped in the temple. Lord Jagannath is the Parwsa Deva of the temple.

Cuttack Chandi Temple
Cuttack

Katak Chandi Temple, an ancient temple dedicated to Goddess Chandi, the presiding deity of Cuttack, Odisha is located nearby the banks of Mahanadi River. The goddess popularly called as Maa Katak Chandi, has four hands holding Paasha (noose), Ankusha (goad), gestures to ward off fear (Abhaya), and granting boon (Varada). She is worshiped as Bhuvaneshvari Mahavidya (the queen of universe) . In Cuttack, people regard Maa Katak Chandi as 'The Living Goddess'.

Dakshinakali Temple
Biragobindapur, Puri

Located 10 km away from Puri, this temple is famous for the belief of devotees on the profound blessings of Kali, the revered deity. Several Sakta temples are located inside and outside Jagannath temple and Puri is consider as a center of Vaisnavism as well as a Sakti pitha. This temple is a Sakta temple dedicated to goddess Kali. Kali Puja is the famous rituals in this temple. All devotees gathered here, they pray in this temple, offer puja and darshan during Kali Puja.

Maa Kandhuni Devi temple
Sorada, Ganjam, Odisha

Ganjam is a district of villages, where every village has a Gram Devati (village Goddess) temple that is worshipped and responsible for all round security and prosperity of the villagers. The history of Shakti worship in Ganjam can be traced from the early centuries of Christian era, when the autochthonous deities of the tribal's (like Sthambhesvari or Khambesvari, Vyaghradevi, Kandhunidevi etc.) were anthropomorphized into the Brahmanical pantheon. In fact, the indigenous Sakta goddesses have been worshipped by the tribal and folk communities since times immemorial, but the Shakti cult

is mostly discussed from the view point of Brahmanical religion. Sorada has a confluence of temples, churches and mosques. The goddess Kandhuni Devi of Surada in the district of Ganjam is another example of a tribal deity being hinduised. Her origin may be assigned to the hoary antiquity. But she was popularized by the patron kings of Surada (a branch of the Bhanjas). She has no iconography, but is worshipped as a Hindu goddess by the Kandha priest. She is revered by the people of all castes and creed and is widely popular in Ganjam district. It is interesting that she was confined only to Sorada. As the name indicates she was originally the goddess of the Kandhas.

    The first Maa Kandhuni Devi temple was built at Padareisuni. But as Maa was the tutelary deity of "Surada Royal Family", Raja Sandhadhanu Singh also established Maa Kandhuni Devi's temple at Sorada for daily worship.

Buddhanath Temple
Balipatna, Garedipanchan, Odisha

The 12th-century Buddhanath Temple is a Hindu temple dedicated to the god Shiva. The temple is in the village of Garedi Panchana in the block of Balipatna, about 22 km (14 miles) away from the city of Bhubaneswar, India. The temple is said to have been built by King Chodaganga Dev of the Somavanshi dynasty. Legend has it that snakebite victims do not die if they are brought to the temple premises.

The temple is built on Tantric principles, particularly the Garedi Yantra. Garedi in Odia, the local language means hypnotism. As the temple architecture and construction is based on Garedi Yantra and it was a well-known centre for tantric studies in the Prachi valley, perhaps the vibrations of the tantric rituals remain in the environment and help snakebite victims. Interestingly, the presiding deity inside

the temple is not a Shiva Linga, but a yoni, or female origin of the 'Shakti'. The absence of the linga in the centre of the temple is a mystery. A smaller temple on the compound, named after Amrutalochani Devi, has an even older deity. Believed to be of tantric origin, the deity inside the Amrutalochani temple has six eyes. It is a two chambered temple with Rekha Deula and a Pidha Jagamohan. It has a Saptaratha Plan.

    Many temples began as Devi temples initially. The addition of male deities and their becoming the main deity is part of the Sanskritization process with Vedic and Brahminical Hinduism taking over the earlier nature and Mother worshipping ancient religious culture in many parts of India. In the East, in Odisha this is especially evident as Dr.K.C.Panigrahi and many others surmise from their studies that Vimala predates Jagannath in Puri and Bhubaneswari predates Lingaraj in Bhubaneswar. Panigrahi says even the temples, not only deities, in the same premises are possibly older than the main central temples!

Gopinath Jiu (Gopaljiu) Temple
Alabol, Balikuda

Alabol, my mother's village is a picturesque hamlet straight out of the story books. Shaded with trees on all sides, quaint houses huddled together; it is immersed in a tranquil aura. Dawn, morning, and mid-day, night: all the same, except for the changes in the air. The air changes the colour of things there. And life whirs by as quiet as a murmur...the pure murmuring of life.

We made our way to the ancestral temple about which we had heard in detail from Ma often. The famous brass idols of Lord Gopal and Radhika date back to the times of Aurangzeb. The head of Dhulia Math, Babaji Shri Vaishnav Maharaj wanted a new abode for the Gods. He entrusted the responsibility of the care of the Gods to the only Karan Vaishnav family of Alabol, the ancestors of my grand-father Late Parashuram Das. Since then, Lord Gopaljiu became the ruling village deity.

The family worships the Lord and celebrates the fairs and festivals as per the guidelines of the Gaya Math. Time stood still that afternoon as we retraced the steps of our ancestors.

Chandaneshwar Shiva Temple
Baleswar, Odisha

The famous Chandaneswar Shiva temple is located at Chandaneshwar, Baleswar, Odisha. Chandaneswar is an acclaimed religious and cultural site of North Odisha. A huge annual fair in the Solar New Year Pana Sankranti, the first day of the Odia calendar, is celebrated on the premises. Many Indian pilgrims visit the temple during this period. During Chadaka Mela (month of April) and Shivaratri, lakhs of pilgrims and devotees from different parts of Odisha , West Bengal, Bihar and other places of India visit this holy shrine to pay obeisance to Lord Chandaneswar.

The temple is small, with a big compound. It has typical Bengali Baro-Chala (twelve eaves) architecture with burnt brick construction. Baro-Chala is a style of temple architecture that originated in Bengal but is rare to find now. The base temple roof has sloping four-eaves of char-chala temple style, topped with a small replica of the temple, on top of that the base temple forming the second layer, followed by an even smaller replica forming the topmost layer. Each roof has four eaves, totalling twelve eaves; thus the name, Baro-Chala. There are small pinnacles on the edges and centre of the main roof. This is also called Pinnacle Style or Ratna style of temple construction.

Ramachandi Temple
Konark, Odisha

Ramachandi Temple is located in a scenic area on the banks of the Kusabhadra River where it flows into the Bay of Bengal. It lies in close proximity to Konark in the Puri District of Odisha. Goddess Ramachandi, the deity of Konark is believed to be the presiding deity of this temple, while others think it to be the temple of Mayadevi, wife of Surya, the Sun God. Ramachandi is reckoned to be one of the most beautiful beaches in Odisha as well as in India.

Ramachandi, the presiding deity is the most benevolent form of Chandi known. It is certainly more ancient than the Sun Temple at Konark. From the religious point of view, it is one of the famous Shakti Pithas of Odisha.

A graceful statue of Chandi, seated on a blooming Lotus flower in a small temple half hidden by sand mounds, on the river mouth of Kushabhadra and the endless Bay of Bengal stretched to eternity, surrounded by a thick growth of Casuarina plantations all around is the scenic magnificence of the place.

A legend regarding the deity is popular among the

locals. Kalapahad, the rebel Hindu Brahmin youth who got converted to Islam, vowed to destroy all the temples of Hindu worship during the 17th century. After destroying the Sun temple, Kalapahad approached Ramachandi temple to destroy it. Then Goddess Ramachandi dressed as a Maluni (a maid servant) asked Kalapahad to wait at the door till she brings water from the river for the Goddess. Kalapahad anxiously waited for a long time to get some cold water. When it was too late and the Maluni did not return he was exhausted and entered inside the temple and found the throne empty. Then he thought the Maluni took away the deity with her and with anger he followed the Maluni. When he reached the bank of the Kushabhadra River, he found the goddess Ramachandi floating in the middle of the river. At that time the river was flooded, so he returned, unable to reach the middle of the river. Then Goddess Ramachandi came in dream of a Panda (priest) and told him to build a temple on the bank of the Kushabhadra River. This place is now known as Ramachandi.

Maa Bhagabati Temple
Banpur, Khurda, Odisha

The presiding deity of this revered temple is Goddess Durga locally called as Bhagabati – the idol depicts the eight armed Goddess and the chopped head of Mahisasura, the vanquished demon.

Maa Bhagavati is the presiding deity of Banapur. The present temple and the Jagamohana are believed to have been built by the Gajapati Maharaja of Puri. The temple of the goddess Bhagabati has earned popularity as a centre of religious activities. At one time, Banapur was the capital of the Sailodhvaba dynasty, responsible for the construction of the ancient group of temples at Bhubaneswar. The large number of Buddhist images discovered at Banapur relates the place to the Vajrayana culture of Buddhism.

BhabakundaleswarTemple
Manikapatna,Brahmagiri, Odisha

Manikapatna is an archaeological site in the state of Odisha. It has been identified with the medieval port of Chelitalo described by the Chinese pilgrim Hiuen Tsang. The site is on the left bank of the Kushabhadra River, at the northern end of the Chilika Lake. Manikapatna is a quaint village, historically significant as it is the place where Manika, a village milkmaid had sold yoghurt to Lord Jagannath and Lord Balabhadra while they were journeying to Kanchi. Two wooden horses which symbolize the horses the deities rode were present near the temple during my visit. Though no-one could actually point out the location where the historic event had occurred, it was somewhere near the anonymously beautiful Bhabakundaleswara temple with a Shiva Linga made of black chlorite. The temple is strategically located on a hillock in Gabakunda village with a breathtaking view of Chilika.

Maa Biraja Temple
Jajpur, Odisha

Jajpur, the ancient capital of Odisha was known as Biraja Kshetra. The Biraja Temple is a historic Hindu temple located in Jajpur, about 125 kilometres north of Bhubaneswar, Odisha. The present temple was built during the 13th century. The principal idol is Devi Durga, who is worshiped as Biraja (Girija), and the temple gave Jajpur the tag of "BirajaKshetra" and "BirajaPeetha". The Durga idol has two hands (dwibhuja), spearing the chest of Mahishasura with one hand and pulling his tail with the other. One of her feet is on a lion, and the other is on Mahishasura's chest. Mahishasura is depicted as a water buffalo. The idol's crown exhibits Ganesha, a crescent moon and a linga.

Biraja Temple is one of the important Maha Shakti Pithas. Here the main idol Durga is worshipped as Girija (Viraja) and Lord Shiva as Jagannath. Sati's navel fell here. Adi Sankara describes the goddess as Girija in his Ashtadasha shakti pitha stuti. Here Maa Biraja Devi is worshipped as Trishakti Mahakali, Mahalakshmi and Mahasaraswati.

The Leaning Temple of Huma
Sambalpur

This abode of Lord Shiva, where he is worshipped as Bimaleshwara is located on the banks of River Mahanadi, 23kilometres from Sambalpur and is a revered place of worship in the region. The unique feature of this temple is its leaning structure; not only is the main sanctum sanctorum in an inclined position, but all the other shrines including the boundary wall are in a leaning position within the temple premises. It is not known if this structure is leaning by design or for some other reason. Although the edifice leans, the pinnacle of the temple is perpendicular to the ground. The plinth of the temple deviates slightly from its original arrangement and as a result the body of the temple has tilted. This tilt has fascinated historians, sculptor's academicians and researchers over time. Interestingly, the main temple is tilted in one direction whereas the other small temples are tilted in other directions. Within the temple complex i.e. within the boundaries of the temple everything is tilted including the boundaries themselves and the villagers and priests says that the angle of inclination has not changed over last forty or fifty years. The tilt may be attributed to geological reasons; the underlying rock may be uneven in structure. The angle of inclination of the tilt has not yet been measured.

As per the records of the British era, the temple dates back to around the middle of the 16th Century AD. The legend of the leaning nature of the temple has many theories attached to it. However if one goes by science, the structure of the temple is based on the simple principle of "Centre of Gravity". For a leaning structure to remain stable its centre of gravity should be located as low as possible & secondly the foundation area should be broad. The temple structure conforms to both.

Huma is a place of pilgrimage and is also visited by tourists to see the different kinds of fish in the holy river. They are said to be docile and eat sweets and other food from the hands of those who bathe close to the temple. During auspicious days they are called by their names and given the prasad of the God. A great fair takes place at the foothills in March every year on the occasion of Shivratri.

Prasanna Purusottam Dev Temple
Tigiria

Prasanna Purusottam Dev Temple of Tigiria is the second highest temple of Odisha and one among the oldest. The temple was built in 1787 by Sri Sankarshan Mandhata & completed by Sri Banamali Champatsingh Mohapatra, the then king of the Tigiria State. The Prasannamani temple is dedicated to the lord Jagannath. The height of the temple is 100ft. In the temple campus major parswa devis and devatas are found like Bimala temple, Laxmi temple, Shiva temple. The temple kitchen and a beautiful garden are also located within the temple premises. This Jagannath temple stands as a best example of kalingan style of architecture, complete with a colossal structure, sculpture and artwork on myriad themes.

The Rath Yatra of Nijigada in Tigiria block of Cuttack is unique for its tradition of pulling chariots. Unlike Puri and other places where the chariots are pulled on the same day, the cars at Prasannamani temple of Nijigada are pulled a day later in keeping with the 300-year-old tradition.

Maa Sarala Temple
Jagatsinghpur, Odisha

The Sarala Temple is a Hindu temple in the district of Jagatsinghpur, Odisha eighty kms from Bhubaneswar. It is one of the eight most famous Shakta shrines of Odisha. Approximately five hundred years old, it was built by the Raja of Manijanga. It is a two-tier temple, having one sanctum and one Jagamohan. The sanctum contains the deity and ten different goddesses sculpted on the wall. Maa Sarala is the goddess of the Vaishnavas and Shaktas. She is  also known as Vak Devi, the Goddess of Knowledge and Wisdom, representing the shiva-shakti cult which evolved from an amalgamation of Shaivism, Shaktism, and Tantric form. It is well documented that Sidheswar Parida a small-time farmer and part time Odia paika was an ardent follower of the Goddess and became Sarala Das, the author of the Odia Mahabharat.

The temple, located in a spacious compound consists of a Deula of pidha order, a Jagmohan or mukhasala with three pidha roofs aligned in a north-south axis and a flat roof mandap. The Anugraha recess has two superimposed figure motifs on each storey. They are filled with erotic kanya motifs, lion motifs on Brahmanical deities. The Devi is eight armed and is placed within a circular medallion decorated with lotus petals.

Maa Tarini Temple
Ghatagaon, Keonjhar

Maa Tarini Temple is a place of great religious significance. Believed to be merciful and benevolent to her devotees, devotees visit from far and wide and offer coconut to Goddess. She is worshipped by priests of tribal origin. Maa is regarded as the presiding deity for all Shakti and Tantra peeths in Odisha. The worship of the Earth as a female embodiment of power is a cultural feature found in different parts of the world.

Maa Tarini is depicted with a red face and two large eyes. The mark in the middle is the symbol for a nose and tilak. This primitive conception is symbolic of simple tribal beliefs. Maa Tarini is the force of life.

Narayani Temple
Ganjam, Odisha

The history of Shaktism is traced from the very beginning of civilization. Shakti, symbolizing power through different phenomena has been a primordial energy in creation. The Vedas, Upanishads, Ramayana, Mahabharata, Tantra and Puranas have lucidly described numerous manifestations of the Shakti and Her significance. Narayani of Ganjam is a prominent Shakti Peeth of Ganjam, Odisha.

The temple of Narayani is situated approximately seventy kms from Berhampur, between Khallikote and Balugaon, atop the Bhalleri Mountain, surrounded by luxuriant Sal and Mango groves. A small perennial spring flows besides the temple. The deity is a ten armed figure of Mahishamardini Durga. In ancient times, the Goddess was being worshipped by the tribals of the region. However, the ex-ruler of Khallikote built a temple for the deity. The style of the temple is a Khakhara Deula, like Vaital Deula. It is supposed to have existed before 12th Century AD.

On the days of Ashokashtami, Mesha Sankranti and Raja Sankranti a large number of devotees gather there to offer worship. Ashokastami is the main festival of Narayani, which continues for three days. The verdant valley, surrounded with Sal and Mango groves, the perennial spring, the view of Chilika lake from the top of the hill are quite enchanting, and attracts a large number of picnickers throughout the year.

The Forgotten Village Temples
(Puri-Brahmagiri)

I was delighted when I got the training assignment of the local community of the eco-tourism sites - coastal villages surrounding Chilika lake. I started from Bhubaneswar early morning to reach the village in good time. Amidst the panoramic beauty of these villages, there were countless village temples, obscure from the public eye, housing gram-devatis/ devatas. I got down from the car and enjoyed the solitude of these temples, far from the madding crowd. A discussion with the few early risers revealed a lot.

The sacred place of worship of the Hindus is the temple or devalaya, the house of the God. A temple is a space, a structure for various religious activities. It is a place of community worship, of communication between gods and devotees. The temples also serve as a promoter of the

arts, a place for divine experience, entertainment, aesthetic relish, social togetherness, as well as home for artistes in the fields of sculpture, painting, music, dance and philosophy.

According to Stella Kramrisch ",Indian temple architecture, in the fullness of its development, establishes in spatial terms an intellectual and actual approach to the Supreme Principle of which the deity is symbolic. The statue is the manifestation (arca-avatara) of the deity through a concrete work of art (murti), and the building is its body and house.

Images are given shape by sculpture and painting, whose inter-relationship expresses in line, proportion and colour the love (bhakti) to which gods and myths owe their existence as aspects of the Absolute."

Temples of Assam

The Hindu sage sees the whole of life. If he does not fight, it is not because he rejects all fighting as futile, but because he has finished his fights. He has overcome all dissensions between himself and the world and is now at rest.

Dr. S Radhakrishnan

Kamakhya Temple
Guwahati

The Kamakhya Temple, also famous as Kamrup-Kamakhya is a Hindu temple dedicated to the mother goddess Kamakhya. One of the oldest of the fifty one Shakti Peethas, it is the main temple in a complex of individual temples dedicated to the ten Mahavidyas: Kali, Tara, Sodashi, Bhuvaneshwari, Bhairavi, Chhinnamasta, Dhumavati, Bagalamukhi, Matangi and Kamalatmika. Among these, Tripurasundari, Matangi and Kamala reside inside the main temple whereas the other seven reside in individual temples. It is an important pilgrimage destination for Hindus, especially tantric worshippers. The association of Buddhism with ancient Assam has a long history. There is evidence to indicate that there was a strong under-current of Tantric Buddhism in this area. There was a mutual exchange of ideas and practices, so much so that aspects in both Hinduism and Vajrayana Buddhism became very similar. The earliest textual reference to Kamarupa as a peetha comes from the Hevajra tantra, one of the oldest Buddhist tantras which came into existence probably in the 8th century C.E.

Sidheswar Devalaya
Sualkuchi, Assam

Sidheswar Devalaya is one of the major temples of this silk village famous for its silk textile. The shrine is dedicated to Lord Shiva. It was renovated by the Ahom king, Shiba Singha. Situated in the south-west part of Sualkuchi on the Sidheswari Hill, this ancient temple was completely isolated when we visited it a fine December afternoon. Long queues can be witnessed especially during the month of 'Bhole Bom', when one can experience a state of trance and divinity. But not now, when the temple was waiting just for us, with a rare regal tranquility. With a terrific view of the Brahmaputra from the top, this is also an ancient Tantric Peeth.

Kedar Temple
Hajo
Kamrup, Assam

An important medieval Shiva temple constructed by King Rajeswar Singha in 1753, it is located on top of Madanchala hillock about thirty-two kms from Guwahati. This is one of the rare Svyambhu (self originated) ling in the Ardhnarishwar (male & female) form of Lord Shiva. This Shiva temple is regarded as one of the ancient temples in the Indian subcontinent. I reached the temple when it was completely deserted, with just one person willing to sell his stories about the ancient legacy of the temple. The winding road leading up towards the temple afforded a terrific view of Hajo. I consider myself truly lucky to have visited this rare site.

"Kailaasarana Shiva Chandramouli Phaneendra
Maathaa Mukutee Zalaalee Kaarunya Sindhu Bhava
Dukha Haaree Thujaveena Shambho Maja Kona Taaree"

Shri Kedareshwar Shivalay
Guwahati, Assam

Situated in close proximity to the famed Kamakhya temple, this quaint temple lies surrounded by shops, buildings & unending chaos. It has rare, ancient statues and a revered Kedareshwar statue worshipped by devotees from all over.

Hayagriv Madhav Temple
Hajo, Assam

This ancient temple, situated atop a hill, has an idol of Lord Vishnu that is similar to the idol of Lord Jagannath in Puri. It is believed that Lord Buddha is believed to have attained Nirvana at this religious site and hence this site is visited by numerous Buddhists, Bhutiyas and Hindus. Hajo is the confluence of Hinduism, Buddhism & Islam. We saw many Muslim devotees inside the temple premises, praying to Madhav. However they are not permitted to enter the sanctum sanctorum. Madhav is believed to be the complete form of Lord Jagannath. The temple authorities were very cordial and we had a peaceful time in this divine ambience.

Temples of Tripura

No Temple made by mortal human hands can ever compare to the Temple made by the Gods themselves. The real temple is this world.

Deserted temples of Udaipur, Tripura.

The Gunabati Group of Temples
Tripura

The 'Gunabati Mandir Gucchha' (Gunabati Group of Temples) lies unsung and forgotten, with very scanty information on its origin. I had the rare opportunity of visiting it during one of my official tours. It was constructed in celebration of Her Highness Maharani Gunabati (wife of Maharaja Govinda Manikya), in 1668 A.D. The three temples have architecture similar to other temples of Tripura .The crown over the stupa on the vestibule is beautifully crafted like a lotus.

Bhuvaneshwari Temple
Udaipur, Tripura

Standing regal on the banks of Gomati River at Udaipur, Bhuvaneswari Temple is one of the ancient temples in Tripura. Built by Maharaja Govinda Manikya during the 17th century, the temple is dedicated to Goddess Bhuvaneswari. Rabindranath Tagore immortalized the Bhuvaneswari temple of Tripura in two of his major plays 'Rajarshi' and 'Bisharjan'. A forgotten temple, hidden in a canopy of greenery, the Bhubaneswari temple is a small structure. We were exhausted by the time we reached there and rested awhile at this green nest.

The flagship Bengal four-chaala temple design is found here. The floral motifs on the core chamber inside the quintessential hut shaped Bengal style place of worship attracts tourists from all over. The Manikya Dynasty established almost all the important Hindu shrines across Tripura. The beautiful temple is perched upon a three-foot elevated porch. There are stupas at the entrance and a core chamber that completes the architecture of the temple. Flower-patterned motifs are the highlights of the temple that adorn the pillars and the stupas.

Tripureshwari Temple

The temple is situated in Udaipur, around fifty five kms from Agartala, Tripura. This five hundred years old temple is the oldest in the Udaipur district. Tripura Sundari Temple is one of the fifty one Sakti Peethas and is the place where the toe of the right foot of Sati fell. Owing to the power emanating from its history, this majestic temple remains flooded by tourists all through the year.

This temple of Kali, built in 1501, is a place where endless animal sacrifices were made. It is believed to be one of the holiest Hindu shrines in the country. It is also known as Matabari and is served by priests in red-robes who minister to the Tripura Sundari.

Temples of South India

Man's history is the history of his journey to the unknown in quest of the realisation of his immortal self – his soul.
Rabindranath Tagore

Shore Temple
Mahabalipuram, Tamil Nadu

Built in the 7th century, Shore Temple depicts the regal artistic tastes of the Pallava dynasty. The temple was constructed during the reign of Rajasimha, when Pallava art was at its best. It is recognized as a World Heritage Site by UNESCO. Perched on a fifty feet square plinth, the pyramidal structure is a typical symbol of Dravidian temple architecture. The Shore Temple generates an exclusive combination of history and natural splendour. The temple was designed to grasp the first rays of the rising sun and to spotlight the waters after sunset. In the words of Percy Brown, Shore Temple serves as "a landmark by day and a beacon by night".

The Airavateswara Temple
Darasuram

Situated close to Thanjavur, built during the reign of Rajaraja Chola II, it is a magnificent structure. This temple along with the Brihadeesvara Temple at Thanjavur and the Gangaikondacholisvaram Temple at Gangaikonda Cholapuram are collectively known as the Great Living Chola Temples, which have been recognized by UNESCO as a World Heritage Site. This temple is dedicated to Lord Shiva. Airavata, Lord Indra's elephant with four tusks and seven trunks, was cursed by Sage Durvasa for disrespecting him. As a result the spotless white elephant ended up with skin discoloration, which was cured only after Airavata took a dip in the sacred waters of this temple. The temple and the presiding deity derive its name from this incident. The spoked chariot wheel, Darasuram c. 1200 C.E. is an architectural work of excellence. The chariot and its wheel are so finely sculpted that they include even the faintest details.

The Brihadeeshwara Temple
Thanjavur, Tamil Nadu

A symbol of the amazing Tamil architecture, this temple was constructed during the reign of the Chola dynasty by Raja Raja Chola and is the largest temple in India. It has been built out of a single piece of granite rock .It is a unique reflection of the splendour and grandeur of the bygone days and gives an insight into the rich culture of the Chola dynasty. The temple is dedicated to Lord Shiva. It is one of the largest temples in India and is an example of Dravidian architecture built by the Chola dynasty. It was built by Rajendra Chola I and completed in 1035 AD.

Brihadeeswara temple is the first complete granite temple in the world. Around 60,000 tons of granite is said to have been used to build the temple. The Brihadeeswara temple along with Airavatesvara temple and Gangaikonda Cholapuram is known as the Great Living Chola Temple and is part of the UNESCO World Heritage Site.

Swamimalai Swaminathaswamy Temple

Kumbakonam, Tamil Nadu

Swamimalai Swaminathaswamy Temple is a Hindu temple located in Swamimalai, dedicated to Murugan. It is situated 5 kms from Kumbakonam on the banks of a tributary of river Cauvery. As per Hindu legend, Muruga, the son of Shiva, extolled the meaning of the Pranava Mantra to his father at this place and hence attained the name Swaminathaswamy. The temple is believed to be in existence from the Sangam period from 2nd century BC and was modified by Parantaka Chola I.

Shiva Temple
Pookkulam, Karanthai
Old Thiruvaiyaru Road,
Thanjavur

"Shiva and Shakti are indistinguishable. They are one. They are the universe. Shiva isn't masculine. Shakti isn't feminine. At the core of their mutual penetration the supreme consciousness opens."

Daniel Odier

This is one of the many ornate Shiva temples dotting the road from Tanjore to Gangaikonda Cholapuram. The dazzling colours and intricate carvings spell out tales of art, rituals and divinity. South Indian temple architecture, also called Dravi?a Style architecture was invariably employed for Hindu temples in Tamil Nadu from the 7th to the 18th century, characterized by its pyramidal, or ku?ina-type, tower.

Temples of Rajasthan

The question is not what you look at but what you see.
Thoreau

The Chaturmukha Jain Temple
Ranakpur, Rajasthan

Dedicated to Tirthankara Adinatha, the temple, with its distinctive domes, shikhara, turrets and cupolas rises majestically from the slope of a hill. Over 1444 marble pillars, carved in exquisite and minute detail, support the temple. The pillars are all differently carved and no two pillars are the same. It is also said that it is impossible to count all the pillars. In the complex, there are several temples including Chaumukha temple, Parsavanath temple, Amba Mata Temple and Surya Temple.

Sahastra/Saas Baahu Temple
Nagda, Rajasthan

"History will be kind to me for I intend to write it."
                                        Winston S. Churchill

This exquisite early 10th century AD temple dedicated to Vishnu sparkles in its rare beauty, despite the ruined state. Constructed according to the concept of "Pancharatha" - Garbhagriha, Antryalaya, Ardhmandap, Mandap, and Varandha, the primary entrance of the temple is known as Kirtimukha. The carvings of Lord Shiva, Goddess Parvati, Chamunda, Kali, Mahishasur Mardini, Krishna, Balram, Parashuram, Brahma and Ram can be seen on the walls, roof plates, and pillars of the temple. Epics from Mahabharata, Ramayana and Lord Krishna's life are depicted on the temple panels.

A temple is a statement in stone with symbolic significance of its own. The Divine is present behind, beneath and beyond the myriad manifestations of life, both mythical and mundane.

Eklingji Temple
Rajasthan

This rare temple is an ancient tantra peeth of India, reflecting the quintessential glory of Mewar. According to the 15th century text Ekalinga Mahatmya, the original temple at Eklingji was constructed in the 8th century by ruler Bappa Rawal. (David Gordon White (2012). The Alchemical Body: Siddha Traditions in Medieval India. University of Chicago Press. ISBN 978-0-226-14934-9.) The original temple and vigraha (idol) were destroyed and lost during invasions Rana Kumbha, in the 15th century, reconstructed the temple, in addition to constructing a Vishnu temple.

Temples of Varanasi

Brahma once weighed the heavens against Kashi. And Kashi, being heavier, sank while the skies, despite all the gods who lived there, rose upwards.

Adi Shankara, Manikarnikastotram

The Ghats of Varanasi

During my Varanasi sojourn, a visit to the Ghats was the top of the to do list. As I went down the steps to the ghats, I was instantly suffused with chaos, colours and the distinct feeling of having stepped back in time. Varanasi, steeped in history, remains a charm through the bygone centuries and continues to attract tourists from India and across the globe. Its Ghats embody the multiple facets of life, its innumerable temples are the sanctuaries of unending spiritual grace, and the river Ganges which gives the city its meaning is the fountain of life and inspiration for many.

Ghats are the epicentres of all kinds of activities in the city. If there is one place where it is possible to contemplate in solitude, while letting the noisy ambience relegate itself to the background, it is the Ghats. As I crossed the different Ghats, I was almost seeing the kaleidoscope of life, the beginning and the end.

Assi Ghat – located at the southern end of the city of Varanasi.

Manikarnika Ghat – famed as the cremation ground for the Maharajas of Kashi.

Dasasvamedha Ghat - The ancient ghat where Lord Brahma executed ten horses as sacrifice (das-asvamedha).

Jain Ghat – A significant ghat with a fort, named after Chet Singh who fought against Warren Hastings in 1781.

Mahanirvani Ghat - located at one end of Nirvani Ghat, named after Mahanirvani sect of Naga Saints.

Hanuman Ghat – Saint Tulsidas, in the 18th century built a Hanuman temple in this ghat; this name Hanuman Ghat.

Harish Chandra Ghat - Named after King Harish

Chandra, this ghat is also referred to as "Adi Manikarnika", the original cremation ground.

Sitala Ghat – is named after the temple of Sitala

Prayaga Ghat - Named after the temple of Prayagagesvara, this ghat is considered as holy as the place Prayag, as it is at the point of union of the rivers of Ganga, Yamuna and hidden Saraswati.

Tripura Bhairavi Ghat - Named after the temple of Tripura Bhairavi, female counterpart of Tripuresvara.

Bajirao Ghat- is named after Bajirao Peshwa, and is also known as Dattatreya ghat, after the temple of Dattatreyesvara.

Scindhia Ghat - was known initially as Viresvara Ghat.

Mangala Gauri Ghat – is named after Goddess Mangala Gauri, which means the auspicious one.

Panchaganga Ghat - Famous as the confluence of five sacred streams of Ganga, the Yamuna, the Sarswati, the Dhupapapa and the Kirana.

Panchaganga Ghat

Kal Bhairav Temple
Varanasi

This is among the rare, ancient temples of Lord Shiva in Varanasi and has a strong link with the history and culture of the city. Kal Bhairav is the fiercest form of Lord Shiva. The deity is portrayed as wearing garlands made with human skulls. It is believed that death itself is afraid of this form of Lord Shiva. People of Varanasi get permission from the deity before leaving the town for any reason. Anyone visiting Varanasi should visit the temple first and get permission to enter into Varanasi, according to folklore. That is the reason why he is popularly referred to as "Kotwal of Kashi". A narrow lane crowded with shops leads to the temple.

Shri Vishwanath Mandir
Varanasi

I was at the historic Banaras Hindu University in connection with deliberations on "Tourism, Religion and Spiritual journeys."I had the opportunity to visit one of the most famous temples and biggest tourist attractions in the holy city of Varanasi, the Vishwanath Temple. The temple is situated in Banaras Hindu University premises and is dedicated to Lord Shiva. Shri Vishwanath Mandir has the tallest temple tower in the world. Shri Kashi Vishwanath Mandir, was destroyed (and reconstructed) several times; in 1194 by Qutb-ud-din Aibak, between 1447-1458 by Hussain Shah Sharqi and then in 1669 CE by Aurangzeb. In 1930s, Pandit Madan Mohan Malaviya planned to replicate Shri Kashi Vishwanath Mandir in the campus of Banaras Hindu University. The Birla family undertook the construction and foundation was laid in March 1931. Despite the rainy season, it was a hot day and tourists were enjoying lazing around in the campus.

Durga Mandir
Varanasi

Durga Mandir, also known as Durga Kund Mandir, Durga Temple and monkey temple, is one of the most famous temples in the holy city of Varanasi. It is dedicated to Maa Durga. It was constructed in the 18th century by a Bengali Maharani (queen) in the North Indian Nagara style of architecture. The temple is painted red with ochre to match the colours of the central icon of Durga, the goddess of strength and power. Inside the temple, lots of elaborately carved and engraved stones can be found. The temple is made up of many small sikharas conjoined together.

The temple is relatively clean. A number of pundits were found reading scriptures. I also met few astrologers inside the temple precincts. The clear afternoon sky did wonders to the deep red of the temple walls. It was indeed a majestic sight to behold.

Sarnath: Buddhist monastery and place of worship

Sarnath is a holy destination near the confluence of the Ganges and the Varuna rivers in Uttar Pradesh, India. The deer park in Sarnath is where Gautama Buddha first taught the Dhamma, and where the Buddhist Sangha came into existence through the enlightenment of Kondanna.

To account for one of the earliest & also the largest religions of the world, Buddhism has flourished since as far back as the 3rd century BCE, having become a significant religion that went even beyond the borders of India, towards East, South and South East Asia. Sarnath, about 20 Kms from Varanasi, is renowned as the place where the Buddha taught his first few disciples. This sacred place, which Emperor Ashoka tried to immortalize by building the greatest Stupa, succumbed to neglect and became rubble of ruins like many Hindu temples in the vicinity. However, archaeological excavations have unearthed what is left of them, and efforts are on to not only preserve the remnants, but also to find out more details about them. It was a relatively sunny day and we had the entire site of the monastery ruins to ourselves. From Dharmarajika Stupa to Dhamekh, walking amidst the colossal ruins was like taking a stroll back in time.

Chausathi Yogini Temples

"If you are depressed, you are living in the Past. If you are anxious, you are living in the future. If you are at peace you are living in the moment."

– **Lao Tzu**

Chausath Yogini Temple
Chousati (Chausatthi) Ghat
Varanasi

The Kashi Khanda described the ghat and images of Yoginis, and mentioned the two Jala-Tirthas ("water associated sacred spots"). This ghat had privilege to provide shelter to a great Sanskrit scholar Madhusudan Sarasvati (CE 1540-1623). Till the 18th century the main image of the Chausatthi Devi was in the Rana Mahal, a palace nearby, which was later shifted to its present site. Chousati (Chausatthi) Ghat is located south of Dasaswamedh Ghat, next to Digpatiya Ghat. It is named after 64 (chausatha) goddesses. Steep steps lead to the Chausath Yogini Temple. With my deep interest in the Yogini cult, how could I not visit this temple? With the help of the boatman-guide and colleagues, few of us dared the climb up the narrow, steep steps. The narrow alleys housed small, quaint hotels on both sides, with a terrific view of the Ghats and the Ganges. The temple is not hypaethral and has a ceiling now. The Mahut and his family stay on the floor above. The sixty four Yogini statues are also missing. Goddess Kali rules resplendent. Many Hindus come to the temple during the new moon day of the month of Chaitra, an auspicious day when they take a dip in the Ganga.

I stood in the empty temple, imagining the time when Kashi was at its glory and the Chausathi Yoginis stayed in this abode, atop the Ganges.

Yogmaya Temple
Mehrauli, Delhi

A Hindu temple, it is a Shakti Peetha dedicated to the sister of Krishna, and situated close to the Qutb complex earlier known as Yoginipura. According to local priests, this is one of twenty-seven temples destroyed by Mahmud Ghazni and later by Mamluks. It is the only surviving temple belonging to the pre-sultanate period. Hindu king Samrat Vikramaditya Hemu reconstructed the temple and restored it from ruins.

Chausath Yogini Temple
Khajuraho

The construction of the Chausath Yogini temple located at Khajuraho can be dated to approximately 885 CE. It is the earliest extant temple at the Chandela capital, Khajuraho. The temple has been classified as a monument of national importance by the Archaeological Survey of India. In the Khajuraho temple complex, away from the main group of twenty-three sculpted temples, built in elegant Nagara style of architecture, there is a unique open-air rectangular sanctuary, dedicated to the Chausatha or Sixty-four Yoginis. The Sixty-four Yoginis shrine of Khajuraho is an important sanctuary of the Yogini cult that was widespread in the vast region between central India and Odisha in the period circa 900 to 1400 and even later. Three large statues of goddesses, found among the ruins, are now located at the Khajuraho museum. The goddesses have been identified as Brahmani, Maheshvari, and Hingalaja or Mahishamardini. These statues are among the oldest sculptures of Khajuraho. The Durga image of the

central cell of the Khajuraho Yogini sanctuary is inscribed with the label "Hinghalaja". This name brings to mind the famous pitha Hingula where the head or crown (brahmarandhra) of Sati fell, according to the Sakta texts.

The Chausath Yogini Temple
Also known as Ekattarso Mahadeva Temple
Mitaoli village
Morena

Also known as Ekattarso Mahadeva Temple, this Yogini temple is an 11th-century temple located in Morena district in the state of Madhya Pradesh. It is one of the few well-preserved Yogini temples in the country. The temple is formed by a circular wall with 64 chambers and an open mandapa in the centre, separated by a courtyard which is circular in shape, where Shiva is deified. This temple is situated on top of a small hill, and is designed on a circular plan. Constructed on a high plinth, it has pillared cloisters that run around the wall facing an open courtyard. The small cells that form 64 subsidiary shrines have a mandapa in front; while a circular main shrine stands in the middle of the courtyard. The cells and the main shrine are flat

topped, but it is believed that initially each had a shikhara on top. The 64 Yoginis originally placed in the 64 subsidiary shrines are now missing; a Shiva linga has taken their place in each cell. The central shrine also holds a Shivalinga. According to an inscription, the temple was constructed by Maharaja Devapala of the Kacchapagata dynasty, dated VS 1380 (1323 CE).

I crossed the Chambal valley while travelling to this sacred spot. It stands anonymous, in solitary splendour, smothered with wilderness and infested with snakes. I shall never forget the spine-chilling thrill I got when I climbed one step up the hillock and saw a huge python slithering past in its royal gait. The driver consoled me that it was Shiva in disguise. It was poor consolation for me though!

The Chausathi Yogini Temple of Morena has inspired and influenced the architectural style of the Indian Parliament building. The circular shape, apart from its aesthetic excellence has also possibly structural strength and stability to withstand the ravages of time including seismic shocks and tremors.

Chausathi Yogini Temple
Hirapur. Bhubaneswar, Odisha

"We are light and dark, sun and moon, male and female, yin and yang; life is composed of opposites, in a continuing cycle of change.... When you are in the light, don't step back into the darkness. Live in that light, and breathe it in fully."

In this temple, every male deity except Shiva is replaced by a female counterpart including Ganesha. The Yogini Cult, Tantrik in nature and tantra itself, projecting the efficacy of magical rituals and spell, sounds and gestures, is intertwined deeply with rural and tribal traditions. There is a diverse range of attitudes toward the tantric traditions, ranging from viewing it as a path to liberation to the relatively widespread associations of the tantric traditions with sorcery and libertine sexuality. In Hinduism, the tantra tradition is most often associated with its goddess tradition called Shaktism, followed by Shaivism and Vaishnavism.

The Yoginis were believed to impart magical powers to their worshippers:

These powers included:

anima (the ability to become very small),

laghima (the power to levitate and to be able to leave your body at will),

garima (the power to become very heavy),

mahima (the power to become large in size),

isitva (the power to control the body and mind of oneself and others),

parakamya (the power to make others do your biding),

vasitva (the power to control the five elements) and kamavasayitva (the power to be able to fulfill all your desires)

(Das, Adyasha, The Chausathi Yoginis of Hirapur: from Tantra to Tourism, Black Eagles Books, USA, 2018).

The Yoginis of Hirapur are ornately adorned, have captivating appearances, both terrifying and mesmerizing, and offer "life-enhancing energies that bring about fertility, growth, longevity, abundance, material and spiritual well-being. Yoginis are wrathful and sensual, ferocious and seductive, furious and graceful. They hold all sorts of tools and weapons, symbolic of what the practitioner needs on his path—a knife to sever attachments, a goad to nudge us along when we are stuck, a bell to clear negativity, a spear for penetrating insight, a bow and arrow for focus, etc. Their mounts are animals, vegetation, and different potent symbols such as a pot, flames, corpse, or drum that lend their powers and mythological significance to the Yoginis."

Chausathi Yogini Temple
Ranipur Jharial, Odisha

"I have created all worlds at my will, and I dwell within them. I permeate the earth and heaven, all created entities with my greatness, and dwell in them as eternal and infinite consciousness."

Located in Balangir district, the twin villages of Ranipur-Jharial reveal remarkable traces of their ancient heritage. Also known as 'Soma Tirtha' in scriptures, this archaeological site dates back to the 9th/10th century AD. Shaivism, Vaishnavism, Buddhism and Tantricism had a great deal of influence in the region during this period. This hypaethral temple provides a glimpse into the religious and occult practices from the medieval times. The Chausathi Yogini temple of Ranipur Jharial is a unique monument. A hypaethral temple, it has niches to enshrine sixty four yoginis. The hypaethral temples were dedicated to a nature deity believed to promote the fertility of the soil of animals and man. The nature deity was worshipped in open air.

The Temples of Bagan
Myanmar

Bagan is an ancient city in central Myanmar (formerly Burma), southwest of Mandalay. Located on the eastern banks of the Irrawaddy River, it's known for the Bagan Archaeological Area, where more than 2,000 Buddhist monuments tower over green plains.

The magnificent historical Buddhist temples of Bagan are eloquent with a rich historical past. In Bagan, layers of dust and sand over time have peeled off most of the stucco coating of these unique constructions.

For the tourists today, what is visible is the underlying brick structure with a distinct reddish and rusty look. When the rays of the sun hit these monuments, at sunrise and sunset, the visitors are mesmerized by the dark golden patina.

"When you see a beautiful place, you carry it wherever you go"!

Cultural Landscapes: Bagan Temples

Bagan Archaeological Zone, Myanmar

Myanmar's Bagan showcases the largest concentration of Buddhist temples, pagodas and stupas in the world. This archaeological treasure is located on the banks of the Irrawaddy River. The rich remains of over 2,500 monuments along with archaeological vestiges of ancient palaces, well-planned water management systems and fortifications are testimony to the highly evolved and significant Bagan period  from the tenth to the thirteenth centuries CE. Remarkable architectural and artistic excellence is manifested in the exquisite ensembles of monuments with their intricate ornamentation and exquisite mural paintings. Till today, many of these Buddhist monuments are revered. The living traditions are manifested by the festivals, celebrations and rituals performed by the locals, pilgrims and the monks from the numerous monasteries. Presently rundown and in ruins, these priceless sentinels of history are in dire need of restoration. The main motivation for visiting Bagan for foreigners is the authentic cultural experience. Most tourists derive sole satisfaction from visiting the temples and pagodas.

Mahabodhi Temple
Bagan, Myanmar

Mahabodhi Temple is a Buddhist temple located in Bagan, Burma. Dating back to mid-13th century, it was built during the reign of King Htilominlo, and is modelled after the Mahabodhi Temple, which is located in Bihar, India. The temple is a two storey structure, about 43 meters high. The pagoda and its square base are stuccoed and contain depictions of several animals and Nat spirit figures. The lower and upper storey of the Mahabodhi temple contains a large seated Buddha image. On the inner wall is an inscription that provides information about the donation of the land where the temple was built on. The Mahabodhi temple was damaged during the earthquake of 1975, but has been restored since then.

Nanpaya Temple
Bagan

Nanpaya is a Hindu temple located in Myinkaba in Bagan, Burma. The temple is adjacent to the Manuha Temple and was built by captive Thaton Kingdom King Makuta. It was built using mud mortar, stone, and brick, and served as the residence of Manuha. In the central sanctuary the four stone pillars have finely carved sandstone relief figures of the four-faced Brahma. The creator deity is found holding lotus flowers, thought to be offerings to a free-standing Buddha image once situated in the shrine's centre, a theory that dispels the idea that this was ever a Hindu shrine. The sides of the pillars reveal ogre-like heads with open mouths streaming with flowers. During my visit, I had the temple to myself apart from few tourists. The road leading up to the temple is crowded with colourful shops displaying local handicrafts and extremely persuasive sellers.

Payanthonzu Temple
Bagan

The Payathonzu Temple is a Buddhist temple located in the village of Minnanthu in Burma. It is unique in the sense that the temple consists of three temples conjoined through narrow passages. The walls of the corridors and the vaults are covered with beautifully painted and well preserved mural painting. The half decorated middle sanctum and the plain walls of the western temple indicate that the work was abandoned before completion.

"I am not the same, having seen the Bagan moon, lost amidst the poetry of temples..."

Ananda Temple
Bagan

Ananda Temple, located in Bagan, Myanmar is a Buddhist temple built in 1105 AD during the reign of King Kyanzittha of the Pagan Dynasty. It is one of four surviving temples in Bagan, an elegant, symmetrical structure with the layout of a Greek cross.

Htilominlo Temple
Bagan

This temple, built by King Nadaungmya, King Zeya Theinkha
dates back to 1218 A.D. A Buddhist temple located in Bagan, built during the reign of King Htilominlo, 1211-1231, it is three storeys tall, with a height of 46 metres, and built with red brick. Inside the 46-metre-high temple, which is similar in design to Sulamani Temple, there are four Buddhas on the lower and upper floors. Traces of old murals are also still visible. Fragments of the original fine plaster carvings and glazed sandstone decorations have survived on the outside. The doorways feature nice carved reliefs. Several old horoscopes, painted to protect the building from damage can be found on the walls of the temple. Each minute I spent there, I was aware of the utter stillness, the silence and the mystical past that was strewn all around!

Ananda Temple
South-east of Tharabar Gate in Old Bagan.
Bagan, Myanmar

This temple is one of the few remaining examples of Mon architecture; it was damaged during a 1975 earthquake but has been successfully restored. The Ananda Temple is recognized as the best preserved and most revered of Bagan temples.

North Guni Temple
Bagan

The spectacular sunsets at Bagan!

Scattered with poppies, the golden waves of the cornfields waft leisurely in the breeze. The red sun seems to tip below the horizon, and simultaneously an amorous, orange moon is lifted up at the other side. The countless pagodas are awash with a reddish-gold hue that is sheer poetry. The clouds are like great wings of gold, yellow and rose-colour, with a smaller minute sprinkle in one spot, like a shower of glowing stones from a volcano. Instantaneously, the hues change to boundless masses of pink, crimson, scarlet, and purple, further up the dome of the sky. It makes the scary climb along the narrow stairway up to the pagoda suddenly so worthwhile. Despite the teeming crowds, I find my own corner and my very own sunset.

"When the Bagan sun has set, no candle can replace it."

Gub Yauk Gyi - 12th century cave temple
Bagan

This temple is located near Wetkyi-in village, North East of old Bagan and was built by King Kyanzittha. The temple architecture shows Indian influence, particularly the spire which resembles that of another temple in Bagan, the Mahabodhi. Both are fashioned after the Mahabodhi temple of Bodh Gaya in India, the place where the Buddha reached enlightenment some 2,500 years ago. The Gubyaukgyi is a cave temple; the first syllable of the temple's name ("gu") translates to "cave". The interior walls and ceilings are decorated with fragments of ancient mural paintings that depict scenes from the Jataka tales, the stories that recount the previous lives of the Buddha.

Bagan Paintings

UNESCO defines cultural and creative industries as "sectors of organized activity whose principal purpose is the production or reproduction, promotion, distribution and/or commercialization of goods, services and activities of a cultural, artistic or heritage-related nature." This approach emphasizes more than just the industrially made products of human creativity; it makes relevant the entire productive chain, as well as the specific functions of each sector involved in bringing these creations to the public. Painting is called "Panchi" in Myanmar. Myanmar's traditional painting developed with the religion of Buddhism in the Pagan Region. There are also works from the Konbaung period (which ended in the 19th century) and the Ava period. During the Mandalay period in the

19th century many beautiful paintings were done in folding books called purapaik and on canvas.

I found most of these paintings in temple walls, paintings by local artistes displayed attractively and marketed aggressively.

The subtle yet captivating art of sand-painting is blooming in Bagan, as craftsmen become more skilled and the costs of producing the area's famed lacquer-ware becomes prohibitive. Many craftsmen took up painting because it was popular among tourists and was a more mobile way to make a living; a painter can simply roll up his or her merchandise and set up shop at the feet of any interested buyer. Sand paintings, which are typically representational acrylic images painted over a sandy surface layered onto a cotton cloth, are a great medium for local artists because they appeal to both foreign and domestic tourists, said 49-year-old painter Maung Pa.

An artist touching up the painting before sale!

The Temples of Yangon
Myanmar

Chauk Htat Gyi Pagoda
Giant Reclining Buddha of Yangon.

The little known Chaukhtatgyi Temple in Yangon has one of the biggest and most graceful reclining Buddha statues in South East Asia. The very impressive sixty-five meters long and 16 meters high Chauk Htat Gyi Buddha image wears a golden robe; the right arm of the Buddha is supporting the back of the head. The Reclining Buddha image is decorated with vibrant colors, white face, red lips, blue eyes, golden robe and red finger nails.

The soles of the feet contain 108 segments in red and gold colours that reflect images representing the 108 lakshanas or auspicious characteristics of the Buddha.

Shwedagon Pagoda
Yangon

The 99-metre-tall gold-plated pagoda with a diamond studded spire is situated on Singuttara Hill, to the west of Kandawgyi Lake, and dominates the Yangon skyline. Shwedagon Pagoda is the most sacred Buddhist pagoda in Myanmar, as it is believed to contain relics of the four previous Buddhas of the present kalpa. According to legend the pagoda is more than 2,500 years old, dating back to the lifetime of the Buddha, making it the oldest pagoda in Burma. Historical evidence suggests the pagoda was built by the Mon around the 6th century. Since then the Pagoda has been enlarged and renovated many times, and numerous smaller stupas and other structures have been added.

Temples of Cambodia

"Just as a candle cannot burn without fire, man cannot live without a spiritual life".

- Buddha

Angkor Wat

Stretching over a wide expanse of 400 square kilometres, including forested area, Angkor Archaeological Park contains the magnificent remains of many capitals of the Khmer Empire extending from the 9th to the 15th centuries, including the largest pre-industrial city in the world. The most famous are the Temple of Angkor Wat and, at Angkor Thom, the Bayon Temple with its countless sculptural decorations.

Angkor was accorded the status of the World Heritage Site in 1992. Situated in Northwest Cambodia, the landscape is represented by four main elements: tropical forest, cultivated land, villages, and the architectural legacy of the Angkorean period. The Angkor temple ruins, which sprawl across the Unesco-protected Angkor archaeological park, are the country's top tourist destination, with the main temple-city, Angkor Wat, appearing on the Cambodian national flag. Regarded to be the most extensive urban settlement of pre-industrial times, and equipped with a

sophisticated water management system, Angkor's decline has long been a matter of investigation for archaeologists. Angkor (Khmer:"Capital City") was the capital city of Khmer Empire, which flourished from around 9th to 15th centuries. Angkor was a mega-city supporting at least 0.1%of the global population during 1010-1220.

The word Angkor is derived from the Sanskrit nagara, meaning "city". The Angkorian period began in AD 802, when the Khmer Hindu monarch Jayavarman II declared himself a "universal monarch" and "god-king", and continued until the late 14th century. A Khmer rebellion against Siamese authority resulted in the 1431 sacking of Angkor by Ayutthaya, causing its population to migrate south to Longvek. The ruins of Angkor are located amidst forests and farmland north of the Great Lake (Tonlé Sap) and south of the Kulen Hills, near modern-day Siem Reap city. The temples of the Angkor area number over one thousand, ranging in scale from nondescript piles of brick rubble scattered through rice fields to the Angkor Wat, said to be the world's largest single religious monument. Many of the temples at Angkor have been restored, and together, they comprise the most significant site of Khmer architecture. Visitors account for more than two million annually, and the entire expanse, including Angkor Wat and Angkor Thom is collectively protected as a UNESCO World Heritage Site. The popularity of the site among tourists presents multiple challenges to the preservation of the ruins.

The Angkorian period may have begun shortly after 800 AD, when the Khmer King Jayavarman II announced the independence of Kambujadesa (Cambodia) from Java and established his capital of Hariharalaya (now known as Roluos) at the northern end of Tonlé Sap.

It was this interesting background of information that

had me smitten and I had Angkor in my bucket list for a long time. So I set out for this trip with immense excitement. I was with a group of academicians for attending a conference at Siem Reap.

Even more interesting to me was the link of Angkor Wat with Kalinga / Odisha in ancient days. Jayavarman was from the Sailodbhava dynasty of Kalinga, with his forefathers arriving in Cambodia through Java/Indonesia. Mahendragiri of Gajapati district in Kalinga dominates the myth and cultural scenario of Kamboja. The Yogini Apsaras are yet another link. The style of temples of Cambodia is indicative of strong Kalingan influence. Banteya Srei Temple of Cambodia near Angkor has significant similarity to Mukteswar or small Panchayatan style temple complexes of Odisha.

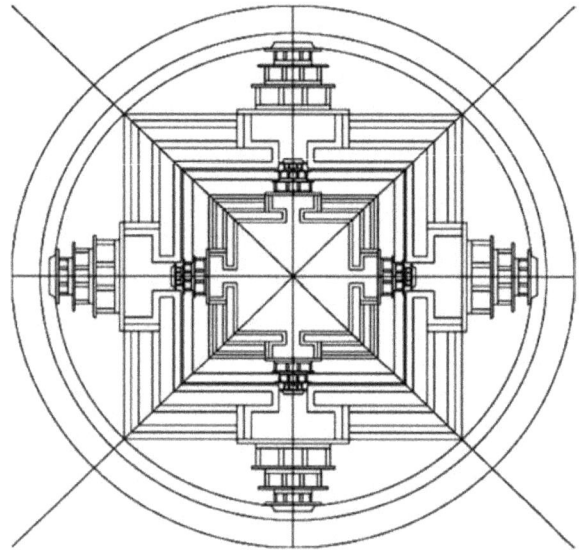

A mandala is a spiritual and ritual symbol in Hinduism and Buddhism, representing the universe. In common use, "mandala" has become a generic term for any diagram, chart or geometric pattern that represents the cosmos metaphysically or symbolically.

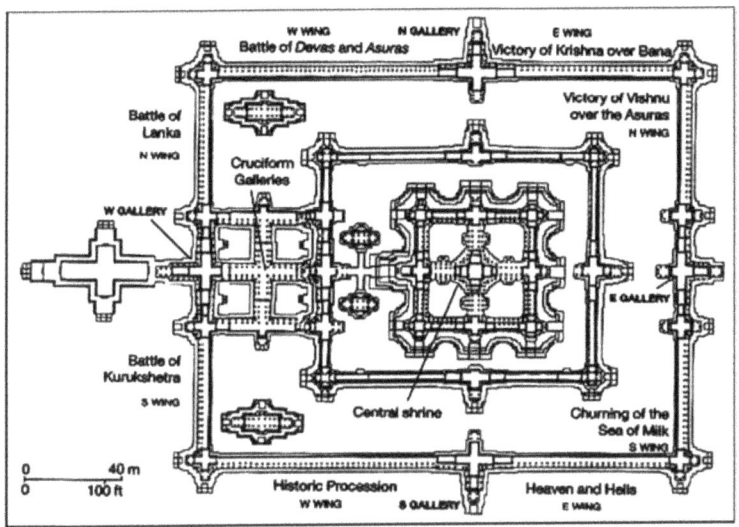

Angkor Wat is arranged around a series of mandala's interlinked to represent ever more complex cosmological and esoteric themes (world-mysteries.com/mystic-places/Cambodia's-)

"Kalinga had maritime relationship with ancient Funan (Kambuja or modern Cambodia). Funan is a name derived from the Chinese term Phnom meaning mountain. (R.C.Majumdar, Kambuja-Desa or An Ancient Hindu Colony in Cambodia, Madras, 1944) The natives of Funan or Cambodia, called Khmers, believed that an Indian rishi osage was their ancestor.As Funan was Indianised by the traders and merchants from the eastern coast of India, the migrants, with the passage of time named a local mountain of Funan as Mahendraparvata after the Mahendra Parvata of Orissa which had god Mahesvara(Gokarnesvara) on it. The famous Angkor-Wat of Cambodia has some affinities with the sikhara of the temples of Orissa and gopuras of the Tamil temples.36 In the Banteay Srei and Prah Khan temples of Cambodia, the mullioned openings are very splendid and in their 'pattern and intention'are akin to the contemporary temples of Bhubaneswar in Orissa. (P.Brown,

India Architecture, (Buddhist and Hindu Periods), Bombay (Taraporevala Sons and Co. Pvt.Ltd.), 1971)"

After arriving, as we glided through a sleepy, dusk-smeared Siem Reap, little did I know about the majestic spread of Angkor awaiting us. Travel blogs, books and websites have over-sold the destination. But nothing had prepared us for the regal beauty of Angkor. A sentinel of the past, it sprawled across acres of land, surrounded by a jungle of trees on all sides. I was awe-struck, silent, lost in my own thoughts.

The colossal ruins of the Angkor temple, zigzagging over the Unesco-protected Angkor archaeological park, are Cambodia's top tourist destination. As already seen in other temples, in various parts of the world, the lions stood guard at the entry point. Cultural depictions of lions have been found in European, African and Asian countries. From Persia to Rome, the lion has been considered a symbol of the sun god Mithra, whilst the Etruscan lion with wings guards the entrance of the Temple Mountain at Troy. In Islam, Muhammad's son-in-law and cousin was referred to as the Lion of God, and a lion headed angel is one of four beings that supports Allah's throne.

The lion is also deeply ingrained in Buddhism, frequently pictured with bodhisattvas who guide people to the path of enlightenment, and Manjusri, a bodhisattva who is symbolic of transcendental wisdom is frequently on the back of a lion. The lion is not merely present across the major religions; it also suggests links or commonalities to the roots of many religions. For Jews, the lion is a symbol of messianic promise and redemption. This has parallels to both ancient civilizations and Christianity.

(http://lionalert.org/page/Lion_Depiction_Across_Ancient_and_Modern_Religions)

Angkor Wat as Mt.Meru:

What struck me most was the staggering size of Angkor, the earthly representation of Mt.Meru. An aerial view of Angkor Wat reveals that the expansive enclosure wall of the temple, which separates the sacred temple grounds from the protective moat that surrounds the entire complex. The temple is comprised of three galleries (a passageway running along the length of the temple) with a central sanctuary, marked by five stone towers. The five stone towers are intended to mimic the five mountain ranges of Mt. Meru—the mythical home of the gods, for both Hindus and Buddhists. The temple mountain as an architectural design was invented in Southeast Asia. Southeast Asian architects quite literally envisioned temples dedicated to Hindu gods on earth as a representation of Mt. Meru. The galleries and the empty spaces that they created between one another and the moat are envisioned as the mountain ranges and oceans that surround Mt. Meru. Mt. Meru is not only home to the gods; it is also considered an axis-mundi. An axis-mundi is a cosmic or world axis that connects heaven and earth. In designing Angkor Wat in this way, King Suryavarman II and his architects intended for the temple to serve as the supreme abode for Vishnu. Similarly, the symbolism of Angkor Wat serving as an axis mundi was intended to demonstrate the Angkor Kingdom's and the king's central place in the universe. In addition to envisioning Angkor Wat as Mt. Meru on earth, the temple's architects, of whom we know nothing, also ingeniously designed the temple so that embedded in the temple's construction is a map of the cosmos (mandala) as well as a historical record of the temple's patron. (https://www.khanacademy.org/humanities/ap-art-history/southeast-se-asia/cambodia-art/a/angkor-wat)

In the Kings vying with each other to be better than their ancestors, Angkor rose to become the world's largest religious complex. I was fascinated by the many headed Nagas seen all over Cambodia, and at the entry point of Angkor, also, notably the naga balustrades. The fascinating apsaras, the quiet presence of Yogini- apsaras, the moat running all around all contributed to a delightful experience.

The amalgamation of Hindu iconography in this Buddhist kingdom was noticeable. Khmer adaptations of Ganesha and Hanuman were present all over the city, and both the Ramayana (known as the Reamker in Cambodia) and Mahabharata were significant in popular imagery. In Angkor Wat, Hindu deities, including a statue of Vishnu at the entrance now worshipped as a Buddhist shrine dominate.

Angkor had been a dream destination for me ever since I had discovered it in books and blogs. It was an indescribable feeling, watching a dream destination take shape before my eyes.

Angkor Wat: a Mandala

The layout of Angkor Wat is arranged to make it one big sacred mandala. Styled like a symmetrical mandala, the Angkor Wat has several correspondences in numbers and shapes. In total, there are 108 lotus bud shaped towers, a sacred number to both Hindi and Buddhists. Mandala's were designed so that every proportion, space, area, ratio, length, breadth and height meant something deeper relating to Hindu cosmology. The fundamental/governing shape in all mandalas was a square, with concentric circles and T shaped gates on each face, all framing the mysterious centre point. Khmer Architects enlarged and reduced concentric squares, circles and triangles to achieve radial balance and to assure their designs were harmonically balanced, in all parts.

A mandala is a spiritual and ritual symbol in Hinduism and Buddhism, representing the universe. In common use, "mandala" has become a generic term for any diagram, chart or geometric pattern that represents the cosmos metaphysically or symbolically.

Drawn as I am, unfailingly, to the romance of ruins and old monuments, Angkor appealed to me almost like it was a primordial connection. As I saw it outlined against the pale morning sky, it was visually breathtaking, the stone lotus on top of the pyramid like temple. Such a colossal structure dedicated to the celebration of religion. Or was it the arrogance of Kings and monarchs to assume God-like images?

"Temple is a place of beauty, a place of revelation".

Angkor is one of the most important archaeological sites in South-East Asia. Angkor is dedicated to Lord Vishnu, the Lord of preservation.

Ta Prohm Temple
(The Tomb Raider Temple)

This famous temple is part of the Angkor Wat Complex, a UNESCO World Heritage Site. During my visit I was amazed by the spectacular ruins of this enchanting temple, swallowed by the majestic trees of the jungle. Beautiful corridors, stone walls are forever intertwined by the spectacular maze of gigantic tree roots. Originally known as Rajavihara (Monastery of the King), Ta Prohm was a Buddhist temple dedicated to the mother of King Jayavarman VII. There are majestic doorways at Ta Prohm, the sacred destination. Doors are special, because the more doors you open to the mysteries of life, or sacred knowledge, the smaller you feel. Our visit to Ta Prohm was in the late afternoon. It was  apparently built as a Mahayana Buddhist monastery and university. I was surprised by the massive invasion of the temple complex by plants mostly of silk cotton tree or banyans. It appeared that nature and architecture were locked in an eternal battle there. The sanctuary is built around the huge, elevated stone face of Prajnaparamita, the personification of wisdom, whose features were modelled after those of the king's mother. Ta Prohm's popularity has soared in recent years along with the rest of the Angkor complex, but especially because of its appearance in the movie Lara Croft: Tomb Raider.

Banteay Srei
The citadel of women
Cambodia

Originally called "Tribhuvanamahesvara", Banteay Srei is a small Hindu Shiva temple but is the most ornate; the temple walls, lintels and pediments exquisitely decorated. One of the most elaborate temples at Angkor, the 10th-century seat of worship is famous for its pinkish sandstone and intricate three-dimensional wall carvings which lend it a uniqueness seldom found in other structures.

Banteay Srei is quite miniature in size, compared to other temples in Angkor. One of the smallest sites at Angkor, Banteay Srei is also called The Jewel of Khmer Art, the Pink Temple, and The Lady Temple.

Banteay Srei's meaning is "Citadel of the Women". Theories suggest that the intricacy of Banteay Srei could have been done only by a woman. The red sandstone used for constructing the temple gives it its characteristic pinkish hue. That's why Banteay Srei is sometimes called "The Pink Temple".

Bayon Temple
Cambodia

The Bayon Temple is unbelievably beautiful and admired among the various structures in the Angkor Wat Archaeological Park. At one time, it was located centrally in the ancient city of Angkor Thom. Famed the world over for its towers with gentle smiling faces, the Bayon Temple continues to be one of the
most sought after destination for tourists. It was a hot, humid day when we visited and certain parts of the temple were in ruins and quite precarious to climb. Several theories abound that regarding the many faces depicted in the temple. Some scholars opine that they represent 'King Jayavarman VII,' Conflicting with this, there are opinions that represent the 'Bodhisattva,' making the Bayon Temple a reflection of both Jayavarman and Buddha. It saddened us to see the heaps of rubble lying as remnants of beautiful

temples, stone temples rolling helplessly on that historic soil. From gates decorated with elephant trunks, Gods and demons, faces of Avalokiteshwar, we were mesmerized by all we saw. As the temple was built in several layers, we had to do a lot of climbing up and down. Life size Buddha statues on the outside of the temple led to the Elephant terrace. King Jayavarman's viewing platform became ours that day, for those moments we were there. Where he looked at the return of his victorious armies, we looked at each other and undeniably agreed that we had the better option to the terrace of the leper king.

The Devata yogini trail- Cambodia
Yogini's / Apsaras at Angkor Wat.

An ancient Khmer image of a Tantric yogini –beautiful, wildly fierce sacred women– is a clue to Tantric rituals in Cambodia.

Temples of Indonesia

To encounter the sacred is to be alive at the deepest center of human existence. Sacred places are the truest definitions of the earth; they stand for the earth immediately and forever.

N.Scott Momaday

Borobudur Temple Compounds
Yogyakarta

This famous Buddhist temple, dating from the 8th and 9th centuries, is located in central Java. It was built in three tiers: a pyramidal base with five concentric square terraces, the trunk of a cone with three circular platforms and, at the top, a monumental stupa. The walls and balustrades are decorated with fine low reliefs. Around the circular platforms are 72 openwork stupas, each containing a statue of the Buddha. The monument was restored with UNESCO's help in the 1970s.

The temple consists of nine layered platforms, six square and three circular, topped by a central dome. The temple is decorated with 2,672 relief panels and 504 Buddha statues. The central dome is surrounded by 72 Buddha statues, each seated inside a perforated stupa. The journey for pilgrims begins at the base of the monument, follows a path around the monument and ascends to the top through three levels symbolic of Buddhist cosmology: Kamadhatu (the world of desire), Rupadhatu (the world of forms) and Arupadhatu (the world of formlessness).

Candi Prambanan Temple
Indonesia

Candi Prambanan is a 9th-century Hindu temple compound in Central Java, Indonesia, dedicated to the Trimurti, the expression of God as the Creator, the Preserver and the Destroyer. A UNESCO World Heritage Site, in almost any other country a magnificent ancient monument on the scale of Prambanan would quickly be designated a national symbol. In Indonesia though it is somewhat overshadowed by the even more awe-inspiring Borobudur temple situated close to it. The two sites are quite different in style with the Hindu Prambanan Temple being a collection of sharp, jaggedly sculpted towers in contrast to the vast horizontal bulk of Buddhist Borobudur.

Temples of Egypt

Man, know yourself... and you shalt know the gods.

- Egyptian Proverbs

The Great Sphinx of Giza
Nazlet El-Semman, Al Haram
Giza Governorate, Cairo, Egypt

I had dreamt about visiting Egypt ever since I had read about it in my 4th standard at school. The fascinating history of this great civilization was the primary reason I wanted to visit this destination. The Great Sphinx of Giza is a sculpture of a recumbent lion with the head of an Egyptian king, carved out of limestone on the Giza plateau probably

in the reign of King Khafre (2558-2532 BCE) during the period of the Old Kingdom of Egypt. Facing the rising sun, it is located on the Giza plateau, on the west bank of the Nile River. Egyptian rulers worshipped it as a symbol of the sun god, calling it Hor-Em-Akhet ("Horus of the Horizon"). The Sphinx sits in part on the necropolis of ancient Memphis, the seat of power for the pharaohs, a short distance from three large pyramids – the Great Pyramid of Khufu (Cheops), Khafre (Chephren) and Menkaura (Mycerinus).

In Greek tradition, the sphinx has the head of a woman, the haunches of a lion, and the wings of a bird. She is mythically portrayed as treacherous and merciless. Those who cannot answer her riddle suffer a fate typical in such mythological stories, as they are killed and eaten by this ravenous monster.

It was one of the most awesome experiences, standing in the sizzling heat and looking at this amazing wonder, at history spread all around.

Temple of Luxor & Karnak

Travelling to Egypt has been one of my fondest dreams come true. I saw the pages of my history book come alive as the train pulled into Luxor, the most important archaeological site in Egypt. My mother accompanied me on this trip and I had the advantage of sharing my admiration with her.

The Luxor and Karnak temples are the remnants of Thebes, Egypt's flourishing capital from the 20th century BC. I passed the silent, enormous statues of Ramesses II and Tutankhamon, the sentinels of the past. Luxor Temple was the setting for the elaborate rituals of the Opet festival, which reconciled the human and divine traits of the Pharaoh. A boulevard of imposing sphinxes led to the much grander Karnak Temple.

Deciphering the enigma of Luxor Temple can be surprisingly difficult. The temple is not dedicated to the cult of a specific deity, which would have its own orthodoxy, but to an abstract concept of kingship, and the Royal Ka itself. The temple was constructed over the span of two hundred years with the oversight of various kings from both the eighteenth and nineteenth dynasties.(Continuity at Luxor Temple, Matthew Unroh)

Karnak Temple
Luxor

The Karnak Temple Complex is a vast combination of ruined temples, chapels, and other buildings near Luxor. It lends its name to the nearby, modern village of El-Karnak. The complex is a huge, sprawling site and is the second most visited historical site in Egypt after the Giza Pyramids near Cairo. It consists of four main parts – the precincts of Amun-Re, Mut, Montu, and the dismantled Temple of Amenhotep IV. The original temple was destroyed and was restored to some extent by Hatshepsut.

The massive temple complex of Karnak was the principal religious centre of the god Amun-Re in Thebes during the New Kingdom (which lasted from 1550 until 1070 B.C.E.). The complex remains one of the largest religious complexes in the world. However, Karnak was not just one temple dedicated to one god—it held not only the main precinct to the god Amun-Re—but also the precincts of the gods Mut and Montu. (Dr. Elizabeth Cummins)

Temples of Sri Lanka

Seek peacefully, you will find.
Proverb

The Temple of the Sacred Tooth Relic

Kandy, Sri Lanka

Considered to be an immensely significant place of religion for Buddhists, the Temple of the Sacred Tooth Relic attracts global tourists as well as monks and Buddhists from Thailand, China, Nepal and various other destinations. Situated at Kandy, the temple is unique for a priceless treasure, one of the most important relics to have been conserved – the tooth of the Buddha! This world heritage site enjoys a unique identity and conveys an architectural language all its own. The sacred tooth is conserved in an encasing that appears like a stupa, kept inside a number of similar encasements. The temple houses several shrines, museums and temples tourists can visit. It is locally called Sri Dalada Maligawa

The Forgotten Goddesses

The Forgotten Goddesses Vinayaki

This elephant-headed goddess, the female avatar of Ganesha is also considered as one of the shaktis or yoginis of Parvati. Vinayaki is an elephant-headed Hindu Goddess. She is known by various names — Vainayaki, Gajanani ("elephant-faced"), Vighneshvari ("Mistress of obstacles") and Ganeshani. These identifications have defined her as the Shakti of Ganesha. (Mundkur)

A unique representation of Vinayaki is found in the tantric seat of worship, the Chausathi Yogini temple, Hirapur, Odisha. Here, she symbolizes one of the 64 Yoginis, a sacred feminine force. In a shrine of the Thanumalayan temple, Kanyakumari is the stone sculpture of a reticent, little-known goddess. Seated cross-legged in Sukhasana, this four-armed goddess has a battle-axe in her upper-left hand and a conch in the lower left hand. In her two right hands, she carries a vase and a staff, around which she entwines her long trunk. She is the venerated female elephant-headed goddess, Vinayaki or Ganeshini, whose origins have been ignored by most writings on Hindu mythology.

The Forgotten Goddess Varuni
The Indian goddess of wine
Varuni, She-Who-Encompasses.

The meaning of this name is probably connected with the Sanskrit madhu, 'honey'. Related Sanskrit words seem to be Madyam, 'intoxicating liquor', used in worship of the Saktis, Divine-Energies, and Madugha, a plant yielding a honey-like substance used for creating love spells and in nuptial ceremonies; it is chewed by debators to ensure success, the same concept expressed in the English phrase: 'honey-tongued'.

In this picture, she accompanies her husband Varuna, the god associated with skies and the seas. Varuni, also known as Varunani is described in Rigveda. She emerged from the Samudra manthan, during churning of the Amrita.

Forgotten Goddess USHA

Ushas is a Vedic goddess of dawn in Hinduism. She frequently appears in the Rigvedic hymns. Goddess Usha symbolizes dawn; she is the daughter of the sky, the creator of the light, who rouses all life. She stirs awake all creatures, and makes the birds of air fly up. Borne on a hundred chariots, she yokes her steed before the arrival of the sun and is never, ever late. Loved by the Asvins, sister of gods, she eludes the Sun who pursues her always. She is not just the harbinger of light but hope, happiness, wealth and all the good things ;  Goddess of light and beauty, whom the Rishis of ancient times invoked for their protection.

In contemporary Hinduism, the revered Gayatri mantra is a daily reminder of Ushas Sri Aurobindo states Ushas is "the medium of the awakening, the activity and the growth of the other gods; she is the first condition of the Vedic realization. By her increasing illumination the whole nature of man is clarified; through her [mankind] arrives at the Truth, through her he enjoys [Truth's] beatitude." An exalted goddess in the Rig Veda , she is less prominent in post-Rigvedic texts. She is often spoken of in the plural, "the Dawns."

Ushas is regionally worshipped during the festival of Chhath Puja, in Bihar and Uttar Pradesh, and in Nepal.

The Mother Goddess

In my sojourn of temples in India and other countries, I have found many temples extolling the virtues of the Mother Goddess, a composite figure encompassing different aspects of the female deity in contrasting incarnations. A mother goddess is a goddess who represents, or is a personification of nature, motherhood, fertility, creation, destruction or who embodies the bounty of the Earth. When equated with the Earth or the natural world, such goddesses are sometimes referred to as Mother Earth or as the Earth Mother. In the very old Indian cultures, the venerated mother goddess was Shakti, the source of all energy in the universe. Some of the manifestations worshipped in ancient temples were associated with natural forces like Ushas, (Vedic Goddess of dawn), and Goddess Ganga, (the sacred river Ganga personified as Goddess).Later in time, she was subsumed in the patriarchal Hindu myth as the consort of Shiva. In this role too, she has been worshipped in various incarnations - benign forms like Sati or Parvati of the terrifying warrior Goddesses like Durga and Kali.

The Goddess Concept
The Gorgons (Syracuse)
Sicily

also known as Medusa and her two sisters, were common decorative motifs on temples beginning in the eighth century B.C. and reaching their peak of popularity in the sixth century B.C. Their image has been found to decorate various parts of the temples across Sicily, Southern Italy, Crete, and the Greek mainland.The Gorgons were a trio of mythological women associated with Greek mythology named Stheno, Euryale, and Medusa. The name of Medusa means "ruling one", and the term gorgos in general means "terrible" and "fierce".The daughters of Phorcys and Ceto, they are not entirely human, instead possessing various monstrous appearances and qualities. They are also the sisters of the Graeae, mythological women/creatures whose names were Dino, Pephredo, and Enyo. Their earliest appearance was in the Greek epic writings of Homer, specifically within the Iliad, dating to approximately 750 BCE, with multiple references to their beings being made in later centuries.

The author in different Temples

Bagan

Sampurna Jaleswar Temple, Bhubaneswar

Tamil Nadu

Brihadeeswarar Temple , Thanjavur

Bibliography

P.Brown, India Architecture, (Buddhist and Hindu Periods), Bombay (Taraporevala Sons and Co. Pvt.Ltd.), 1971

Continuity at Luxor Temple, Matthew Unroh

Das,Adyasha, The Chausathi Yoginis of Hirapur: from Tantra to Tourism, Black Eagles Books, USA, 2018).
David Gordon White (2012). The Alchemical Body: Siddha Traditions in Medieval India. University of Chicago Press. ISBN 978-0-226-14934-9.

Essay by Dr. Elizabeth Cummins

Mishra, Kishore Ch. (2000) "Religious Syncretism and the Jagannath Cult in Orissa" Proceedings of the Indian History Congress Vol. 61:1, pg. 144-151.

Majumdar, R.C., Kambuja-Desa or An Ancient Hindu Colony in Cambodia, Madras, 1944

BLACK EAGLE BOOKS

www.blackeaglebooks.org
info@blackeaglebooks.org

Black Eagle Books, an independent publisher, was founded as a nonprofit organization in April, 2019. It is our mission to connect and engage the Indian diaspora and the world at large with the best of works of world literature published on a collaborative platform, with special emphasis on foregrounding Contemporary Classics and New Writing.

www.ingramcontent.com/pod-product-compliance
Lightning Source LLC
Chambersburg PA
CBHW042126100526
44587CB00026B/4189